Peacekeeping:
Police, Prisons,
and Violence

Peacekeeping: Police, Prisons, and Violence

Hans Toch
State University of New York
at Albany

Lexington Books
D.C. Heath and Company
Lexington, Massachusetts
Toronto

Library of Congress Cataloging in Publication Data

Toch, Hans.
    Peacekeeping: police, prisons, and violence.

    Includes bibliographical references and index.   ˌ
    1. Police. 2. Prisons. 3. Violence. I. Title.
HV7921.T63   363.2   76-5622
ISBN 0-669-00652-1

Second printing, May 1979

Published simultaneously in Canada

Printed in the United States of America

International Standard Book Number: 0-669-00652-1

Library of Congress Catalog Card Number: 76-5622

Contents

Preface

This book deals with violence—violence encountered in prisons and by the police. It examines the violence that prisons and the police must cope with as they go about their business of reducing violence for the rest of us.

Police violence and prison violence would seem to be very different problems that might be examined conjointly only because the two institutions are part of the criminal justice enterprise, and of interest to the same experts. But there are more substantial links. The police are tentacles of social control, and prisons must face bitter opposition and resistance. Where credentials fail to rather not do, such as go to jail and stay there. This means that police and prisons must face formal opposition and resistance. Where credentials fail to persuade recalcitrant clients, violence becomes a risk. Police officers and prison guards are trained to expect violence and to use it themselves when necessary.

Among the persons whom police and prisons control are some who have used violence (or are very likely to use violence) against others. Such persons must be neutralized and treated. We assume that police and prison staff are experts in recognizing cues to violence, and in dealing with it as a short-term and long-term problem. We also assume that correctional and police personnel can handle the danger entailed in day-to-day contact and cohabitation with violent men.

Other links between police and prisons are less obvious, and it is one of the purposes of this book to trace them. In chapter 1, I sketch out some themes that seem to run through criminal justice agencies, which may invite and shape violence. I also try to explore institutional reforms addressed to such themes, which may reduce violence for the police and in prisons.

The bulk of this book talks about police–suspect confrontations, about violence in prisons, and about efforts to deal with future conflict and to reduce it. In each chapter I begin with a view of the problem as it appears at first glance, and amend this portrait to make it fit reality, as best we know it from the research literature, and from experience.

This book, however, is not a dispassionate portrait. It builds and documents a view. I assume, for example, that violence breeds violence, and that control makes controllers vulnerable. I assume that the most "direct" approaches to violence backfire. I see violence as an inevitable risk for criminal justice agencies that define their mission as "fighting crime." I see it reduced only through organizational change, by a redefinition of mission toward peacekeeping. I see violence minimized where police reach out, and where prisons strive toward some staff-inmate community.

ix

Acknowledgments

The preparation of this book was supported under Contract ADM-42-74-48 (SM) from the Department of Health, Education and Welfare. I am indebted to Thomas Lalley and to Saleem Shah of the Center for Studies of Crime and Delinquency, NIMH, for their careful reading of the manuscript, and for invaluable editorial assistance. Opinions expressed are my own, however, and do not reflect the views of NIMH or of the Center for Studies in Crime and Delinquency.

1 Introduction

Persons inflict physical injury on each other in different social contexts and settings. Some violence, such as barroom brawls, occurs in small groups; some, such as child abuse involving a single parent and child, features two participants. Other violent acts—riots, for instance—comprise large crowds.[a] These types of violence have been surveyed, thought about, and discussed.

There is little written, however, about violence that occurs in formal organizations. We do know that some enterprises, such as death camps and wartime armies, exist to inflict violence. Their destructiveness may be understood as a corporate product, and in-house production experts can discuss the output, expense, and efficiency of violence. The need for the violence is established and carried through by staff. Hiroshima and Buchenwald are thus enterprises in which executives and employees did their assigned jobs.[b]

Even violence-oriented organizations may distinguish between destructiveness that subserves their ends, and that which does not. In some instances (e.g., in death camps) constraints are negligible; in others there are rules, which may be stretched or violated. Strictness varies with the times. Some war crimes were lauded and rewarded at the time they occurred. With bad publicity, a "routine" act can easily be redefined as transcending or violating goals of war, and the perpetrator turns from a faithful soldier into an unlicensed, free-lance killer; he becomes a man who blatantly exercised misguided initiative to "improve" on his orders.

Violence in Nonviolent Organizations

The situation is more complicated for organizations that are not violence-oriented, but which allow for the use of violence in support of nonviolent goals. Some sports teams, for example, are flexible about the use of bloodthirsty

---

[a]The term *violence* denotes the inflicting of physical harm or injury on one or more persons. Ball-Rokeach [5] points out that "in everyday language, 'violence' typically refers to *illegitimate* uses of force" (emphasis added). She notes that through such a relativistic definition "research on violence . . . often suffers by witting or unwitting adoption of pre-judgments" (p. 101). Like Ball-Rokeach, I assume that the term "violence" may be used to describe *any* act in which a person injures another person physically.

[b]The issues related to this type of violence can be described in terms of people's willingness to obey superiors in inflicting violence. Stanley Milgram supplies an excellent overview of this process in his book *Obedience to Authority* [89].

1

tactics. Some schools permit teachers to punish disruptive students. So long as the occasion or provocation for the act of violence is documented and as long as the damage is within bounds, the perpetrator can be seen as furthering a cause. He sees himself and is seen by others as taking needed measures to help his team win or to insure quality education. His violent impact (such as broken ribs or difficulties experienced by the victim in sitting down) can be viewed as an insignificant means to a significant end. All the user of violence need do is point to the fact that the harm inflicted did not transcend the amount of destructiveness informally or legally permitted, and deemed necessary to accomplish organizational consequences.[c] The criteria invoked have to do with accepted means–ends relationships, and drawing blood or using harsh language may serve as upper limits of the permissible means to similar ends in two sister organizations. As a rule there is stress on *minimizing* the uses of violence to the amount that is needed to reach goals that cannot be reached in other ways. This stress is partly due to the organization's self-image, and partly to the fact that the outside world tends to frown on the unfettered use of force.

Individual discretion in most organizations cannot be controlled bindingly, tightly, or concretely. The average person tries to live at peace with his superiors by trying to "keep them off his back." Administrators must accept this condition of leadership. The man on the front line must always be allowed to interpret rules, and the situations to which he applies them. The men who make rules, such as commissioners and boards, are not present where the rules are applied. They cannot assess the "need" for concrete reactions to individual situations. This point holds for the *instrumental* use of violence. The occasion for violence and the results of violence are generally only obvious to the user of violence, to his victim, and to immediate spectators.

Controlling Violence

Where an organization's rule maker assumes that violence will be curbed by his rules, he ignores other pressures and motives. What occurs is that the organization provides *one set of forces* that governs the use or nonuse of violence. Other forces arise from the situation in which violence is provoked, from the motives of the user, and from the social network that surrounds the aggressor and his target. The locker rooms of nonviolent organizations may bristle with calls for "no holds barred" action. Some persons test the limits of their discretion more sparingly or generously than others. Some define conduct calling for a brisk

---

[c]The Metropolitan Applied Research Center notes that "in the absence of laws prohibiting corporal punishment of students, court decisions have held that such punishment must be administered without malice, be reasonable in the light of the child's age, sex, size and physical strength, be proportionate to the child's offense, and be employed to enforce reasonable rules" [88, p. 19].

tackle or a slap narrowly; others, broadly. Some men use violence reluctantly; others, with pleasure. Since situations calling for violence are interpersonal, some dispensers of violence may even provoke, or contribute to, the problem to which they respond. A teacher may inspire ridicule, for instance, and then suppress it.

Rule and Reality

Teachers, hospital attendants, policemen, and prison guards are empowered to use force to prevent or interrupt injury or disruption to themselves, to clients, and to outsiders.

While organizations may need violence to counter violence, they must then face the violence potential in their own ranks, and monitoring such potential carries problems. Violence restrictions must always be vague due to the difficulty of spelling out in advance the situations in which violence may be needed, or in which it should be avoided. It is easy, for example, to tell psychiatric attendants that as *a last resort,* disruptive patients may be restrained or immobilized. But this does not specify the meaning of "disruptive," nor spell out options that one prefers to physical restraint, nor does it describe preferred ways of getting the patient into a camisole. Such determinations are made on the scene—in the recreation room or dormitory—and on short notice. A patient curses and lifts a chair; he is large and looks wild; others are restive. There is no time to consult a supervisor or wait for the doctor. An action is taken and a precedent set.

Given the generality of most restrictive rules, the legitimacy of deployed violence must often be ascertained *after the fact.* It is then that a decision can be made about whether the use of violence fit organizational prescriptions, or contravened them.

Monitoring Violence

Routine reviews of organizational incidents are rare, because such reviews cause embarrassment, and affect morale and loyalty. A violent incident becomes visible mostly where there is public concern, internal conflict, or support for a victim. If a hospital patient dies, if he complains to an influential relative, if someone invokes the ACLU or if the patient's ward explodes in riot, an inquiry is likely. The organization then faces the onus of suspected complicity as a sponsor of violence. It could be labelled "brutal" or "bloodthirsty": the incident could show attendants empowered to beat patients, for instance, as a standard practice or policy.

To protect itself, the organization can always deny the incident, justify it, or play it down. Failing these options, it can shift the blame by *completely personalizing* the violence. To do so, the user of force must be exposed as individually violent. Better still, he must be violent in violation of rules—which presumes, of course, that the rules have been clear.

"Violent" staff members do cast suspicion on those who hired, trained, or supervised them. But this relationship may at worst denote carelessness. Prompt reactions, such as firing the culprit, show good faith.

An illustration is provided by a Bronx school in which deans had been punishing disruptive students. This regime was started by new administrators, facing a difficult student body. As these men saw it, to "teach" problem students required severe discipline.[d] According to later testimony,

alleged past disorders in the school including acts of vandalism had brought about conditions in the school that obstructed learning. Legitimate fears of parents that their children would be deprived of opportunities for learning and achievement in a "chaotic" school situation or become involved in delinquent behavior caused many parents to regard the establishment of law and order in the school as the first priority [88, pp. 4-5].

Provisions in the bylaws of the New York City Board of Education forbid corporal punishment. Despite such rules, paddling of students routinely took place at the Bronx school. For a time, no one seemed to object; parents felt that "corporal punishment for those students who misbehaved was not too high a price to pay for the order that had been achieved" [88, p. 5].

One staff member (a guidance counselor) ultimately complained, and was "warned that his actions might cause him trouble, including an action for libel" [88, p. 6]. He faced unpopularity and harassment. Ignoring threats, he approached the press, and described prevailing practices, complete with evidence in the shape of a wooden paddle. Then—and no earlier—the organization acted, and reaffirmed its "rules." Directives were issued asking principals to observe the board's ban on punishment. The Bronx school denied all charges, but also requested a change in the rules. Ultimately, as further testimony rolled in, the denials stopped. Blame was now attached, and the deans were depicted as unprofessional, and were disciplined. The principal was reprimanded.

The fact remained that violence had been used routinely, as a matter of course, and with social support. Teachers and students had viewed the practice as "normal." After the scandal, members of the community still expressed fear

that criticism of the principal or placing a check on his power to administer discipline would engulf the school in the disorder and violence which were all

---

[d]In his school violence report to the Committee on the Judiciary, Senator Birch Bayh [12] notes that "many teachers feel that only when seriously disruptive students are properly controlled can the remainder of the school community continue the task of education" (p. 12). Senator Bayh documents the conclusion that the "level of [school] violence and vandalism is reaching crisis proportions which seriously threaten the ability of our educational system to carry out its primary function" (p. 3).

too common in public schools in poor areas. Their first concern was that their children should learn enough to achieve greater opportunities than they had known, and that their children should not be truant, misbehave in school or become delinquent [88, p. 11].

This episode is less complex than others, because the participants were high level. Usually, when staff are singled out as violent, they are members of lower echelon front line groups. These groups feel understandably threatened when administrative action is taken. If one member is blamed for on-the-job exercises of force, why not others later? The rules exist, but so do tangible "threats to peace." Staff must intervene—sometimes without notice—to protect or to prevent disturbances. A serious problem arises, as staff see it, when administrators who were not present at the scene can subsequently raise questions about the need to have acted.

Distinctions between "good" and "bad" staff are of little help. The "good" staff member of today can see himself labelled "bad" or "violent" tomorrow. Differentiations of "good" and "bad" conduct are drawn by nonfront-line personnel, whereas the soldier faces exigencies in combat. If invoking the organization's rules does not insure front-line staff automatic support or "backing," the rules are seen as empty. Remote men are deemed to use technicalities against those who do the organization's real work conscientiously.

Often, crises are the highlights of one's work. In some jobs, the decision to use violence is the least routine and most "professional" decision one makes. What one does the rest of the time, such as changing bedpans or patrolling the halls, confers little status. Restraining the Dangerous may be the principal measure of one's worth. Violence is also the means to control unpredictable personal danger. If authority to deploy violence is reviewable, this may mean less protection against physical harm, and a more degrading assignment.

The fact remains that when violent incidents are publicized, organizations must generally act to pin blame on individuals and to highlight their destructive motives or propensities. The point holds not only for staff, but for client violence.

While staff violence may label an organization "brutal," client violence classifies it as negligent. There is a presumption, for example, that schools can protect their students from getting stabbed in hallways, and that hospitals can insure that patients not jump from windows. This presumption exists even where schools are populated by rival fighting gangs and hospitals are full of despondent patients with records of suicide attempts.

Organizations often try to maintain low profiles about client violence. School fights end in infirmaries and principal's offices; suicidal gestures become statistics. It is the dramatic event, or the outsider, that makes violence news. A fatal stabbing or a suicide's spouse's complaints raise questions about violence levels, and about the institution's ability to police itself.

In response to charges of negligence, organizations may argue that their clients are uncontrollable; or they may talk about their limited capability for monitoring and controlling clients. Either of these claims can boomerang. Clients who are labelled dangerous may feel called upon to act dangerous, and control claims explode when violence reoccurs after the organization arms itself to the teeth.

Organizational survival may hinge on managing not *primary violence,* but *secondary violence*—violence arising from the organization's *response to violence.* In the long run, the latter may be more likely than primary violence to reduce community acceptance, morale of staff, and receptivity of clients. It is not hard to cope with conflict; it is very difficult to curb escalation. By permitting the use of violence, an organization may keep the peace and pursue its goals. It must inevitably, however, discover that through the use of force, new problems are created as others are solved.

Police and Prison Violence

Police departments and prisons are clear instances of organizations in which force is necessary and appropriate to achieving goals. For the police and sometimes for the prison, killing marks the limit of permissible intervention. Prisons use extreme forms of restraint to control harm or self-harm. Prisons also bear responsibility for high levels of violence by inmates against other inmates.

Police and prison violence and its control are of immense practical importance, because (1) penal institutions and police departments are public agencies, whose conduct reflects on society generally, (2) the legal and physical power, and the potential for abuse by police officers and prison staff is substantial, (3) much police and prison activity is of limited visibility—not easily subject to outside control, and (4) the consequence of free-lance police or prison violence can polarize the community and destroy public confidence in government.

Criminal justice organizations must obviously be more oriented toward violence concerns than other human service enterprises. They presume to deal with a violence-prone clientele, and have the mandate of protecting us from violent crimes. This mandate is reflected in an emphasis on potential danger.

Given the presumption of danger for the police and in prisons, these organizations have a problem with *the management of fear.* Staff must deal with their fears of dangerous clients, clients with their fears of all-powerful staff, and some clients with their fears of other clients. Although such concerns help to insure personal safety, their appropriateness hinges on the closeness of fit between fear and threats. But fear in prisons and among police may be artificially fanned. It may be fed through ego-boosting war stories and tales of horror. It may be nurtured by romanticized conceptions of one's role. And it may be rewarded by a premium placed on bravery. Men may be led to provoke others by overcompensating for their fears. They may spread pretenses of bravery. They may generate conflict by statements of "fight or flight" philosophy.

There are also fear-enhancing pressures and supports from the formal organization. Organizations know that staff who are responsible for the safety of others must build up sensitivity to danger cues. In the process men may be unwittingly trained to feel vulnerable and unprotected.

Police, prison staff, and inmates also tend to disproportionately spring from working-class backgrounds, and they are accustomed to regard physical prowess (and willingness to fight) as *measures of manly worth.* This view may include an emphasis on the virtue of appearing self-sufficient and acting tough. One consequence is a reluctance to face and to surface feelings such as doubt or fear which break up the facade. There may be a deemphasis of open communication and of deescalation in conflict. Where egos are threatened, men may react in ways, such as swaggering, posturing, or blustering, which enhance the chances of violence.

Police and prisons also furnish chances for *confusing one's private reactions with expressions of one's role.* Staff and clients may fight personal battles, such as demonstrations of toughness, or redressed hurts to their self-esteem, under color of law (or lawlessness); they may also take organizational problems and convert them into personal crusades. Inmates are "harassed" by "racist" guards; officers are "baited" by "militants" or "trouble makers." Violence may thus be *officially* invoked to deal with self-made conflicts, and *unofficially* used for organizationally relevant ends.

An *implicit combat and warfare* model is also a feature in prisons and among police. Staff and clients tend to view each other as enemies, and tend to regard their peers as trench mates. Breaks in client and staff ranks are seen as openings to the enemy. Although a peer may be violent, he is also a comrade-in-arms who deserves protection or silence. Questions of solidarity, of maintaining a common front, become strong concerns. Exaggerations of enemy militance and malevolence become supports for morale.

Personal safety needs run strong against a backdrop of organizational insecurity. Control measures against violence (as defenses against exaggerated threats) always fall short of what men feel is needed.

An obsession with security also motivates people to tolerate conduct to which they might otherwise object. If violent staff are allowed to keep their jobs, this means that other jobs (including one's own) are more secure. If violent inmates go unpunished, other inmates are more certain of their own status and benefits. Protecting violent peers can help a man feel safe from incursions by outsiders or superiors.

To the extent to which police and prison administrators officially deplore violence and extol civil rights, community relations or public relations, they send *double messages* down their ranks. A "double message" creates a climate that confuses people about what is expected of them.

Among police, one of the "messages" is the shape of the job, which consists of calls for service, the need to get along with the community, and the strictures of the law. The other "message" is the stress on aggressive policing. The organization may tend to lionize the man who engages in combat; it rewards and promotes the tough cop. The presumption that such norms can be reconciled with the job (in "well rounded policing") takes no note of the difficulty of working out a formula for appropriate conduct. There is surprise when the officers usually end up resolving cross-messages by complaining that they are "damned if they do and damned if they don't."

Prison guards often feel that their superiors favor inmates and hold guards in lower esteem than burglars. This view derives partly from administrators' efforts to maximize custodial and treatment concerns. The guard knows that his time is spent in work that is not stressed in his custodial mandate, such as responding to inmate requests for services.

Inmates are similarly pressed. They must peacefully co-exist, but their status (or safety) hinges on advertised aggressiveness. The *composite* inmate may not be the kindly-but-tough stereotype, but a man with problems. If the inmate responds to antiviolence norms he is "weak"; if he uses violence, he risks both his parole and peace of mind.

Neither staff nor clients of typical agencies have individual autonomy. Inmates live with inmates; police have partners. Staff work in groups and face client groups. Such facts have consequences for conduct. Because men *need to belong,* they do what they must to "buy" acceptance, tolerance, or status. If the peer group favors toughness it may motivate aggressive behavior despite personal preferences or organizational rules. Differences in the person's desire to belong (dependency needs) can be as important in producing violence as more direct motives such as personal explosiveness.

Where group norms that favor violence exist,[e] it is hard to assign personal blame for conduct. Controls that are aimed at shared conduct bring shared defensive reactions; these may transform a peer culture into a contraculture,[f] a monolithic, hostile, and obdurate group. Such a group may gain status and permanence from organization of its own, such as a police benevolent association, a custodial officer union, or a prisoner's rights group.

Organizational Climate

Some prisons and police departments are more subculturally dominated than others. Some have more "manliness" concerns, and more problems with fear,

---

[e]The connotations of a specific "subculture of violence" have been delineated by Wolfgang and Ferracuti [196]. The concept describes groups in which violence is permissively viewed, or is prescribed as a "solution" for a wide range of problems.

[f]The term "contraculture" was coined by Milton Yinger. A *contraculture* is a subculture defined as holding "inverse or counter values (opposed to those of the surrounding society) in face of serious frustration or conflict" [198, p. 626].

rule stretching, insecurity, role conflicts, and client–staff hostility than do others. But no prison or police department is devoid of social reinforcement for some staff and inmate violence.

This is not to say that criminal justice agencies are riddled with blood and gore. Concerns and needs that feed violence are balanced and neutralized by other norms. Legal and organizational rules, professional goals, and idealistic motives all reduce the potential for violence. The problem is to keep these norms from being overwhelmed, and to make them dominant and effective.

The pages that follow suggest one road to this goal. This prescription is one that subverts rather than confronts violence-promotive norms. It implies that the organizational goals of police and prisons can be modified to remove the occasions for, and to reduce the urgency of, concerns such as "manliness," militance, and toughness. Realigning goals is a more ambitious strategy than more limited change prescriptions, which include techniques such as screening, training, and discipline. But we have known many such gambits to fail. We have also known why they failed. We have known that strategies which apply discrete pressure to any change targets may increase tension and promote resistances [75].

But pragmatic considerations are not solely at issue here. We know that police and prisons have heretofore unexploited potential, which lies mostly in the human services area. This fact stands out for us against the crime-fighting or warehousing stance currently in evidence. We see it in police units speeding in aid of the infirm, the troubled, and the weak. We see it in the work of prison staff amid the confusion of tiers and the bustle of yards, where guards provide solace, empathy, and reassurance to inmates. Such events are deviations from traditionalist norms, but they also exemplify a tangible direction, a new tradition, which may be reshaping the criminal justice system.

In the following chapters, I will view separately the problems of police and prisons; try to describe the forms violence takes for each organization, for its clients, and its staff, and then turn to program implications and trends. Finally, I will try to link program ideas into a more general model. If this conception can be implemented, it may not only reduce violence, but may accommodate crucial needs and values of criminal justice clients and staff.

2 The Shape of Police Violence

For the police, violence is an occupational risk, and force is an occupational tool. The public is most aware of the fact as it relates to the use of *extreme* violence by—and against—the police. Such violence makes news. Typical *New York Times* stories include opening paragraphs such as,

New Brunswick, N.J. (UPI)—Two state policemen were shot and seriously wounded early Sunday when they stopped a car with South Carolina license plates for a routine check. A short time later one suspect was killed and two others captured at a nearby girls school [102].

The Police Department's Civilian Complaint Review Board is investigating charges that a Brooklyn policeman shot and critically wounded an auto-theft suspect Sunday afternoon out of personal dislike [103].

Detroit, Jan. 16—A man shot and killed two police officers and wounded two others today during a gun battle that began shortly after the police responded to a call about a domestic quarrel [117].

Sometimes publicized police violence is not only dramatic, but unusually brutal, and is apt to inspire calls for action:

Dallas (UPI)—Three sheriff's deputies, their hands tied behind their backs, were shot and killed Monday as they fled across the Trinity River bottomland from two burglary suspects who had disarmed them [100].

Dallas, July 24 (AP)—A 12 year-old boy, handcuffed and seated next to a policeman in the front seat of a squad car, was shot to death today by an officer seated behind him, the police said [111].

Extreme incidents of violence exert an intolerably disproportionate cost in life and limb, but they are also socially disruptive. Men who start their working day or night sensitized to the possibility, however remote, of death or serious injury must face the management of their fear, and suspects who view police as sources of serious victimization are apt to be apprehensive of encounters with officers.[a] When fears are played out against a backdrop of ethnic feelings—since

---

[a]Police representatives often claim that the policeman "puts his life on the line seven days a week." The number of officers killed, although it has increased over the years, now averages 100 men. This provides the average officer a 3,500 to one chance of surviving the year—better odds than those faced by taxi drivers and coal miners. The probabilities, of course, are not evenly distributed, and officers assigned to high-crime areas are in greater danger than others.

most police officers are white, and many suspects nonwhite—violent incidents can lead to an ethnic "warfare model."

Symptomatic of the impact of extreme violence is the impetus it provides to the escalation of police armament. Illustrative is a *New York Times* article headed "Baltimore Responds to Officer's Death with Shotgun Squad." This story points out that the new heavily armed Baltimore squad "marks a major shift from the approach adopted in the late 1960's of avoiding major demonstrations of force in an effort to prevent confrontations between the Black community and the police" [114]. Unlike bullet-proof vests, which protect the wearer, police shotguns are offensive weapons intended for retribution rather than self-defense. Thus a president of the New York Patrolman's Benevolent Association (who complained that "on the very day New York Police Commissioner Patrick V. Murphy was rejecting the P.B.A.'s request for the issuance of heavier weapons, two Milwaukee policemen were shot and killed") conceded that shotguns might not help ambushed officers. On the other hand,

shotguns in the back-up cars right behind them would have been devastating to the animals who were doing the ambushing. One revolutionary with a large hole blown through him would have been a marvelous deterrent to the next nut who thinks it's a good idea to shoot at cops [105].

Even where police organizations stand fast against such a call to arms, rank-and-file feelings can produce informal changes in conduct. Do-it-yourself measures can include the carrying of unauthorized weapons and heavy duty ammunition. Given strong fear among officers, such practices can become prevalent in the face of explicit prohibitions. In the words of one New York patrolman,

we have been told that if we get caught in the car with anything other than a .38, we'll have charges brought against us. But it's better to be judged by 12 men than to be carried by six. That's the motto around here [104].

A generic problem with reactions to extreme violence is that countermeasures can have a wholesale, irreversible impact on large population segments. An example is our current system of airport security measures, which—while reducing hijacking— forces the deployment of many thousands of private police personnel (in demeaning and nonchallenging capacities) at astronomical expense to passengers. The airport *as an institution* is thus significantly changed in undesirable ways in response to threats posed by small numbers of threatening individuals.

With respect to the police as an institution, violence-inspired changes can

---

Charges of police genocide ("Stop Killer Cops") stand on poorer statistical grounds. If we use conservative arrest figures (those reported to the FBI) the average felon has 1 in 20,000 chances of being killed by an officer—or 350 deaths to 7,000,000 arrests.

pull the profession away from progress achieved over the last decades. A militaristic officer is not the clear-eyed generalist depicted in the law enforcement literature. He becomes an expert on the appropriate use of force, rather than a sophisticated practitioner of police services. And his societal impact can take increasing social control connotations.

The Milwaukee deaths referred to by the PBA president provide an example of the effect of extreme violence on police. Ten days after the incident, the *New York Times* noted, "this city (Milwaukee) has grown increasingly tense." A black city official charged that "the real horror of this situation is that all Blacks are being treated as though they were guilty and had a part in Wednesday's events" [106]. Similar polarization resulted fom police response to an officer's death in Pittsburgh. The public safety superintendent pointed out that "people have to understand this is a special situation and police have broad powers in going after a fleeing felon." The testimony of citizens confirmed that "broad powers" were being deployed in the incident's aftermath. Such deployment included the use of battering rams to smash doors of apartments in which free entry was allegedly being offered [122]. Although Pittsburgh police practices may not have amounted to wholesale harassment (as was charged by some) they stimulated considerable bitterness in the community.

Portraits of more long-term impact are furnished elsewhere. The most dramatic instance was a controversy surrounding police practices in the city of Detroit. Here, a "law and order" police unit (STRESS) became an election issue that divided public opinion, principally along ethnic lines. According to the *New York Times,*

Its friends see STRESS officers as shock troops of the war in the streets, a corps of urban heroes who are catching criminals and bringing law and order to the asphalt frontier.

Its critics—blacks in particular—see STRESS as a gang of murderers and thugs who, operating under the aegis of the law, beat, shoot, harass, intimidate and kill innocent citizens. Often, they say, it is a case of white policemen against black citizens [108].

The STRESS story illustrates a sequence more complex than that of police reactions producing public reactions. The issue is one of a *pattern* of police *violence.* The STRESS unit "was reputed to shoot first and talk later." During its first year its 100 members "accounted for nearly 40 percent of all killings by Detroit's 5,000-man police force during that period" [108]. The point here is that a particular organizational response to violent crime significantly increased the chances of violence by the organization as a whole.

Violence-inspired responses may not only create new violence for the police and the community, but for individual officers and citizens. Officers may be more likely to kill suspects who make "furtive movements" towards guns that never materialize. If a stimulus is ambiguous, an officer is more likely to infer the possibility of danger if his perceptions are conditioned by fear. Reactions to low probability violence (if it is extreme enough) can increase the chances of violent reactions, which in turn create occasions for fear. Riots illustrate this process, because they often break out when police incidents are viewed by hostile spectators against a backdrop of past police–citizen confrontations [184].

Ethnicity is a contributing variable to violence, because a disproportionate number of civilians involved in police violence are nonwhite. Of persons who were killed by police officers, 468 out of 975 identified between 1962 and 1971 were black. Nationally, 60 percent of persons shot by officers are nonwhite [181]. In New York City, where blacks make up 19 percent of the population, they account for 59 percent of fatal police victims [112]. In Detroit, only one citizen of those killed by STRESS was white.

Such data are sometimes translated into inferences about discrimination. This conclusion is not fair, because most persons who are shot by police are involved in serious offenses at the time of the incident [147]. Distributions of known offenses and of arrests show ethnic disproportions similar to those of shootings. In New York, for example, during the period corresponding to the 59 percent police victim figure, 62 percent of persons arrested for violent crimes were black. Moreover, black policemen (who are less likely to be prejudiced, but are more likely to be assigned to high-crime areas) proved to be disproportionately responsible for fatalities involving black suspects [112].

As for public outrage, no instance is known where the occasion for public concern rested on statistical distributions. Fear and anger are stimulated by dramatic encounters in which an officer's misjudgement is at issue, where the offense is minor, where the suspect is young, or where some combination of these factors is present.

The point holds also for police reactions to police fatalities. The concern here is often couched in terms of snipings or premeditated ambushes, which account for some 10 percent of police deaths. Such acts have the most substantial claim to impact, because they are hardest to anticipate, and because they raise the specter of a mysterious conspiracy aimed at the lives of officers.

Every police death, on the other hand, is apt to mobilize both fear and anger. Police funerals are the occasion for well-publicized ceremonials and the subject of emotion-laden interest. The facts of the specific incident (including possible negligence) figure insignificantly in its perception by officers. The point at issue appears to center around feelings of vulnerability, and around group identification with the victim.

Although police violence that results in death may spark feelings of impotence, the criminal justice machinery is comparatively well equipped to react to these events. Discharges of police guns are subject to tight monitoring and review; questionable killings by officers are reacted to as criminal and civil matters, and as departmental problems. Killers of policemen rarely escape conviction or death. Out of 343 known offenders between 1968 and 1970, only 5 remained fugitives by the end of 1971 [182].

Police who kill citizens are not as vulnerable. One reviewer of the situation [70] notes that "of 1500 incidents (of fatal shootings by police) I have been able to discover only three in which criminal prosecution resulted" (p. 164). The same reviewer points out that the information that is available about police deaths is not matched by diligent inquiries into police killing. "Information about incidents where policemen are killed," he tells us, "is easily available (for instance, in the annual reports-issued by the FBI); however, even simple data on police killings are hard to find, and details of these homicidal encounters are extremely difficult to locate" (p. 164). The fact remains that police departments are well informed about shootings by their own men, including off-duty shootings and firearms discharges.

Nonlethal Police Violence

Violence involving injury, but no fatality, occurs frequently between police and public.[b] This kind of violence is hard to control, because it is hard to establish and is difficult to define. Its physical cost is minor, compared to its corrupting and corrosive influence, which is subsurface. In fact, its visibility is generally minimal. Although police assaults involve thousands of daily confrontations, these incidents rarely make news. They are recorded in in-house documents that form part of modest legal proceedings. They are described in police reports, in words such as the following:

Suspect #1 stated "I don't have to show you my license because I haven't done anything wrong, and I think this is pretty Goddamned ridiculous to go stopping people and trying to give tickets during the Christmas season." Complainant informed Suspect #1 that he was required by law to submit his license to a police officer on request, and failure to do so shall result in arrest. Suspect #1 then submitted license to complainant, and stated, "Where am I living, in some Communist country? You're just a snot-nosed brat in a blue jacket." At this time rather than take more oral abuse from suspect, complainant returned to patrol car to write citation, in peace. Complainant was only a short ways through the citation when Suspect #1 came back to complainant's patrol unit.... Complainant ordered suspect back to his vehicle. Suspect refused, stating "you don't tell me what to do, you little b-----d. I am going to get your badge number and fix you." Suspect #1 reached in my window and grasped my badge, trying to rip it off and half pulling complainant out of patrol car. Complainant lifted door handle and kicked open door, knocking Suspect #1 to ground. At this time wit-

---

[b]Assaults on police officers, as reported to the FBI, have steadily averaged 1 for every 5 officers, per annum. Assaults with bodily injury to the officer occur at an average rate of 7 per 100 officers per annum.

ness #1 arrived and helped Complainant put cuffs on Suspect #1. While doing this. Complainant was attacked from behind by Suspect #2, who was cuffed immediately.

Officer observed two male whites 16–18 years. . . . Both appeared to be unsteady on his feet and possibly drunk. Officer pulled his car alongside and while stepping out of the car said "come here fellas." Both continued walking. Offficer said louder "I said come here. Now hold it," whereupon the suspect ran north. . . . Officer pursued suspect and caught him as he was going over the railing of a witness' back porch. As Officer grabbed suspect, the suspect turned and swung at Officer with his right fist. Officer struck suspect twice with baton to subdue him and had to continue to struggle to get suspect handcuffed.[c]

The social science literature relating to police violence is most intensively concerned with violence of this kind, and particularly with the police role in promoting it. Questions of the most practical concern have been sparked by the suspicion that officers sometimes polarize conflict, or use force in excess of that dictated by circumstances or by law. As we shall see, most available data show that few officers are in fact confrontation prone. But the data also suggest that a great many officers tend to protect and support those few officers who often are involved in violence. This latter observation makes the problem of police violence a difficult and challenging one.

Several sources of information have been used to generate data about police violence. One such source is the civilian observer who rides with police, and views police conduct directly. A related strategy is that of interviewing officers about incidents in which police violence was employed. These data sources have been very rich, which suggests that the officers may tend to view their violence as relatively justifiable [144, 145].

Another source of data has been the civilian participant in violent incidents. Police assaulters and assaultees have been interviewed by researchers, and attorneys for such men have provided accounts of civilian versions of police violence. The value of these data is that they supplement the police version with a totally different perspective.

Other data sources are arrest reports and civilian complaints about police. The availability of such data stems from the legal context of police confrontations. For one, assaulting an officer is a clear-cut offense, often more serious than the grounds for arrest—if any—that spark confrontations. When an officer uses violence he is also on more secure grounds (in court, and in his own department) if he can establish that he was subject to a prior attack. This fact is persuasive enough for officers to continue to file charges such as resisting arrest even when their supervisors suspect that a man who frequently arrests people on such grounds may have problems. Similarly, police assaulters sometimes file brutality charges to buttress a case, otherwise tenuous, in court.

---

[c]These two incidents descriptions are excerpted from arrest reports in the files of the Oakland (California) police department.

The Seminal Study of Police Violence

William Westley ranks as a pioneer among students of the police. His work dates two decades back, but its results have been confirmed in more recent investigations. More importantly, Westley proved a sensitive observer, whose portrait of police is sympathetic and plausible.

Westley emphasizes that the policeman's workaday reality—the circumstances under which he encounters the public—is such that it forces the officer to derive a jaundiced view of segments of the public. This outlook has nothing to do with personal motives and attitudes; it arises instead out of the adversary nature of police—citizen interactions. The officer's enforcement role defines him as an unwelcome intruder who is apt to meet hostility from people:

The fight in the bar, the driver in a hurry, the bickering mates, the overtime parker, the cutters of edges and the finders of angles; the underworld—bitter, sarcastic, afraid; none of these find the policeman a pleasant sight. To them he is the law, the interfering one, dangerous and a source of fear. He is the disciplinarian, a symbol in brass and blue, irritating, a personal challenge, an imminent defeat and punishment. To him they are the public, an unpleasant job, a threat, the bad ones, unpleasant and whining, self-concerned, uncooperative, and unjust [191, p. 49].

Westley tells us that when the officer is on the job, he cannot draw subtle distinctions between his role and his feeling as a human being who is disliked and disrespected by other human beings. This contamination can work both ways. The officer invokes his badge where the law is not at issue, or becomes personally involved in matters that call for dispassionate reactions. He may come down hard on men he finds uncongenial or distasteful. He may react to challenges; he may see the police role compromised where he is not shown as much deference or cooperation as he would like.

Persons who treat the officer with disdain become classed as "wise guys." The officer's perception of some civilians as "wise guys," and the issue of receiving (or not receiving) respect, becomes, for Westley, a key force in shaping the policeman's conduct. Other things being equal, the officer is more likely to arrest the man who is disrespectful to him. Arrests take place only partly to enforce the law: premises of morality often play key roles. It may be a critical fact whether a delinquent is seen as a salvageable child, as a "sniveling punk" or as a cop-baiting tough. A drunk calls for different disposition if he is belligerent, repentant, or disarmingly helpless.

Because all police activity is ostensibly exercised on behalf of law, there is need to maintain a pretense of objectivity and legality vis-à-vis the outside (non-police) world. This is especially the case when violence is deployed. When violence is used by some officers to punish "wise guys," other officers tend to keep silent about such incidents, even when it is known that the officers involved acted extralegally. Westley maintains that

Secrecy and silence are among the first rules impressed on the rookie. "Keep your mouth shut, never squeal on a fellow officer, don't be a stool pigeon," is what the rookie has dinned into his ears; it is one of the first things he learns [191].

Westley also argued that since police officers find the public unappreciative, they look to each other for protection, esteem, and understanding. They are thus drawn together into a tight fraternal group, which perpetuates itself by being passed on from one generation to the next. It is passed on partly through formal induction into the police department (the recruit academy), but mostly through work-related contacts between old-timers and new officers. In Westley's words,

Eight hours a day, six days a week, around the clock, they talked with their partners. Long hours between action have to be filled; and the older men, hungry for an audience, use them to advantage. Here the experienced man finds an opportunity to talk about himself as a policeman, about his hardships and happinesses. Here he is expected to talk. His talk makes him feel good— more important, here is someone to whom he is an expert; here he finds none of the boredom of his wife, or the derision of the public, but an eager, subservient listener. Thus, amidst an incessant barrage of warnings as to silence, the recruit is initiated into the experience of the man, the history of the department, the miseries of police work, the advantages of police work, and the gripes and boasting of a long series of men. The older man, who had been long bottled up, who is insecure about himself and the worth of his job, who faces from day to day an unfriendly world, exploits the situation to the full. The rookie proves a psychological asset. This is the training and the initiation [191, pp. 157–58].

Westley's contribution to the police violence literature is a two-fold one. He showed that there were relatively few police officers who were inclined to excessive and repeated use of violence, and that these were men concerned with problems of respect and self-esteem. He described a generous support system for the violence-prone officer in the shape of in-group loyalty, and through norms of secrecy and mutual support. Westley tells us that the police violence problem rests among officers who feel strongly about disrespect and evil, and with the police solidarity that makes the problem officer difficult to identify and to discipline.

In a recent preface to his study, Westley draws a practical inference. Violence, he tells us, must be addressed by involving the police more positively in society, so as to decrease the adversary (in-group, out-group) relationship between most officers and the public they serve. He states that:

Means must be found for integrating the police with the community and for de-escalating their adversarial role. To do this, police organizations must be democratized by involving as many policemen as possible in decision making on all aspects of the department's jobs. Policemen must also be integrated with the community through increased police participation in decision-making bodies. and through public participation in a wide range of police activities [191, p. xvii].

We shall return to this program implication later.

The Police Perspective

Westley postulates a support system for violence in the shape of locker-room norms. Some of these norms, such as the premise that disrespect must be curbed because it makes you look weak, translate into violence when they are taken literally. Other norms, such as the premise that a brother-officer can do no wrong, do not promote violence, but help to protect it. Both sets of norms are impressed on a man by his fellow officers through a process of informal socialization.

Niederhoffer, a sociologist with 20 years service as a police officer, has confirmed and elaborated this point. Like Westley, Niederhoffer maintains that police come to see the law as a tool, and that they often view it very pragmatically. If police meet special circumstances about which they feel strongly, they are especially apt to bend the law to accommodate their aims. Niederhoffer tells us that:

The rookie begins with faith in the system. He tries to follow the book of rules and regulations. Then, he discovers that many cases have repercussions of which the book seems wholly ignorant. He is chastised by his colleagues for being naive enough to follow the book. Gradually he learns to neglect the formal rules and norms and turns elsewhere for direction. Individual interpretation replaces the formal authoritative dictum of the official book and the young policeman is an easy prey to cynicism [133, p. 52–53].

Cynicism may take the form of underenforcement—the norm of leaving well enough alone—or overenforcement—the tradition of acting without basis in law.

Overenforcement sometimes features violence, but so does underenforcement. When potentially troublesome situations are avoided, this reduces the chances of a then-and-there confrontation. But unresolved problems may contribute to violence in the community, and may reinvolve the police at a later (more advanced) stage.

Niederhoffer adds a new dimension to Westley's thesis by calling attention to the fact that socialization within the police does not take uniform hold. Whereas some officers become "hard-nosed," others become service oriented. Assignment may accentuate the differences between groups; it may even polarize them. The "tougher" officers may find themselves in "tougher" situations, which cement and reinforce their outlook.

Documentation for the violence-related impact of police socialization also has been provided by John McNamara [85], who conducted a study of training and its impact on police practices and beliefs.

One unusual feature of the McNamara study is that it not only explores violence-promotive norms, but also describes ways in which police can contribute to violence through lack of social skills. Recruits can become participants in conflicts if they have skill deficits in areas such as

(1) the gathering of an adequate amount of relevant information about a situation and the citizens in it both prior to and during the interaction between the officer and the citizen(s); (2) the clarification of police expectations for the citizen; (3) the exploitation or utilization of the values of the citizen(s) [85, p. 169].

McNamara tells us that officers often provide a citizen with overly restricted alternatives. A suspect may be given no choice other than complying with unacceptable demands or attempting to escape. Where incidents involve spectators, such as friends or relatives of the suspect, officers may take insufficient cognizance of threats they pose to the suspect's reputation or "position of authority." Police may also reinforce a man's feelings of victimization by demonstrating disinterest in him as a person.

A question of "presentation of self" may often be involved. Officers may be enjoined to be "firm and courteous," but may tend to accentuate the former. McNamara recalls that the recruits he encountered often shouted their requests loudly in role playing, expecting to secure compliance. He also mentions that many recruits tended to confuse courtesy with deference, which to them was "unconscionable."

McNamara presents test scores to show that entering police officers are relatively nonpunitive in orientation, and no more authoritarian than other working-class groups. They also voice moderate views about a number of issues related to violence.

McNamara points out that the response patterns of recruits change—sometimes markedly—with time on the force. For example, the view that if an officer does not accept a challenge to fight he gives civilians the feeling that they can "get away with anything" or can "push the police around" increases in popularity over time.

Generally speaking, the recruit's point of view hardens after he leaves recruit training, with increased exposure to "old timers" on the force. McNamara assumes that training fails by not forearming its graduates against such pressures of the locker room. He argues that

this failure seems to be caused by a fear that discussion of beliefs or practices at variance with the position of the administration will be taken by all relevant parties as endorsement of these beliefs or practices. Whether or not this fear was justified, it seemed to have the opposite effect from that intended, in as much as

the recruits later moved closer to positions seen as inappropriate by the administration of the department [85, p. 215].

McNamara points out that the typical recruit academy operates under serious handicaps. For one, it is a house divided, with some staff stressing the use of
force, and others emphasizing its illegality. There is also a fairly pervasive stress
on "common sense," which stipulates skills and attitudes. Moreover, everyone
on the force views the academy as "impractical," and as imparting unrealistic
theory. "It was a common feeling," writes McNamara [85], "that academy personnel must have never actually worked in field units" (p. 248). This perspective
goes hand-in-hand with the assumption that the role of older officers includes
the duty to acquaint recruits with "realities" of policing.

Another factor contributing to impotence is the prevailing cynicism about
"playing it by the book." McNamara [85] talks of consensus in the locker room
on the premise that "efficient police work would be impossible if an officer were
to follow the Rules and Procedures to the letter" (p. 241). One regulation, calling for reports of violations of rules and procedures, was referred to as the "rat
rule."

McNamara not only sees training as poor socialization, but views administrative interventions as poor vehicles of change. Since conduct is not guided by
rules, sharpening orders can have only limited impact.

While McNamara sees administrative moves as doomed by the nature of the
police job, he sees hope for training. Training can be subverted to the extent
that it is unrelated to practices in the field. To close the gap, cognizance must be
taken of the perceived realities to which training must bridge.

The Suspect's View of Police Violence

Paul Chevigny and an ACLU project he headed offered legal representation to
men and women who claimed that they had been assaulted by police. From intensive investigation of numerous such cases, Chevigny tells us that:

Complaints . . . bear out the hypothesis that most such acts arise out of defiance
of authority, or what the police take to be such defiance. A majority of the complaints about force (55 percent), whether authenticated or not, appeared on
their face to involve defiance, and the overwhelming majority of the authenticated complaints were shown to involve such defiance (71 percent) [31, p. 70].

Like Westley, Chevigny feels that officers confuse their private and public
roles. He tells us that police operate on the premise that they must act to redress
disrespect, because failure to do so weakens their authority:

Policemen apparently do see themselves as personifying authority, and a challenge to one of them (or to all of them, as in the case of civilian review) is a

challenge to the Law. Everybody knows that when you defy the Law, you go to jail [31, p. 139].

Perceived defiance of authority can take many forms. Some, such as wrestling the officer for his nightstick, are extreme, while others (such as refusing to move) are minor. A spectator who criticizes an officer at work may be viewed as an agitator; a person who quotes the Bill of Rights may be seen—in context—as a cop hater. Some challenges are verbal, and others are gestures; some are intended, and others, such as a drunk urinating on the station room floor, may not be addressed to the police.

Persons who are more frequently stopped by police have more motivation, and more frequent opportunity to raise questions about the legitimacy of police actions. Middle-class citizens are infrequently involved in police violence, because they are contacted less frequently, and are less prone to defy authority. For the middle class, subservience is compatible with self-esteem; working class perspectives may require a manly show of outrage or defiance.

Like Westley, Chevigny contends that some police violence features contempt for deviants, men such as sex offenders, pushers, or derelicts. Chevigny makes the point that these sorts of incidents (unlike violence generated by disrespect) enjoy little support in the police subculture. Although the officer may protect a colleague who has kicked a handcuffed child molester, he will not afford him respect, nor defend his actions.

A crucial distinction of police violence, says Chevigny, rests in the fact that police file charges against their opponents. Such charges tend to be efforts to defend one's personal loss of control:

Many police abuses take place in front of a crowd of witnesses, and no real attempt is made to conceal the act until criminal charges are filed after it is over. The false criminal charges are a more serious offense by a patrolman and constitute a greater evil than the act of violence itself. The unjustified use of force in front of witnesses when public feeling about police brutality is running as high as it has for the last few years, must be an act performed in a flash of anger; the premeditated act is filing the cover charge [31, p. 73].

Chevigny contends that police departments provide support for violence, by emphasizing arrest criteria of productivity. Although violence may be undesirable, the violent officer is an active officer; it is to the department's interest to help him be productive. It must try not to discourage such a man, even if he is "a bit rough":

The Department seems to have made a decision, poorly articulated to be sure, that an officer is not to be disciplined for acts performed in the line of duty if those acts show initiative and an effort to maintain order. An angry reaction to defiance is thus felt to be one of the more minor of a policeman's failings. The effort to convict a prisoner is likewise to be commended, and shaving the acts a little to bring out that conviction is less reprehensible than avoiding the arrest altogether. The officer is at least showing initiative and the will to make arrests and obtain convictions—as far as the Department is concerned, virtues of a "good cop" [31, p. 67].

Chevigny feels the criminal justice system is generally less concerned about curbing police violence than it may pretend. Judges and prosecutors are reluctant to intervene, in part because the system relegates the dirty work of crime fighting to the police, while preserving its formal legality elsewhere. The public has a similar interest, a similar subconscious view. Its concern for fairness goes hand in hand with a desire for "efficiency," with few questions asked. Police norms do not evolve in vacuity; they have supports outside the police system.

Wertham and Piliavin's [190] classic portrait of black youth gang contacts with the police highlights the awareness that teen-age boys have of police officers' desire for respectful treatment. One gang member summarizes his impressions as follows:

You know what cracks me up about them guys, them cops you know, they think you're supposed to do everything they say just 'cause they're cops. They don't even bother about the books. They just think that because they're cops you're supposed to respect them more than anybody else. Does it say that? Does it say in the books that you're supposed to respect them more than anybody else? No it don't! You're supposed to respect everybody, right? And you're supposed to treat everybody equal. They shouldn't be treated as though they were anything special. You should extend courtesy to them the same as you would to your family, the same as you would to your father and mother. I mean you don't have to go out of your way for them. I mean I don't even say "Sir" to my old man. He doesn't expect me to say "Sir!" What a bunch of phoney dudes [190, p. 97].

Real irony lies in striking parallels between attitudes prevailing in the police and youth gang subcultures; the genesis of violence often hinges on who shows respect, or fails to show respect, for whom. For the youth gang member, a police contact may itself signify lack of respect. If this incursion is aggravated by additional "disrespect," a violent reaction is legitimized:

When a patrolman is polite, he can sometimes mitigate the resentment and the sense of injustice provoked by the situation of suspicion. It is almost as though a new reality had temporarily erased the insult to moral character that was implicit when the patrolman decided to interrogate in the first place. To a large extent, therefore, the issue of whether the authority of the patrolman will be challenged hangs on whether this initial insult is compounded or dissipated during the course of interrogation [190, p. 86].

Gang members have their own version of cynicism, which can make police officers fair game. And like the police, the gang boys find it hard to distinguish between official contacts and personal affronts. This can result in mutual testing, which polarizes resentments and leads to a showdown:

Negro gang members are constantly singled out for interrogation by the police, and the boys develop their own techniques of retaliation. They taunt the police with jibes and threaten their authority with gestures of insolence, as if daring the police to become bigots and bullies in order to defend their honor. Moreover, these techniques of retaliation often do succeed in provoking this response. When suspect after suspect becomes hostile and surly, the police begin to see themselves as representing the law among a people that lack proper respect for it. They too begin to feel maligned, and they seem to become defensively cynical and aggressively moralistic [190, pp. 56-57].

Wertham and Piliavin point out that just as officers have their version of meritorious delinquents, gang members allow for "good cops." A "good cop" holds authority in reserve, but does not abrogate it. He shows understanding and tries mediation. When he intervenes, he has clear cause, but overlooks minutiae. Above all, he must sport a man-to-man stance, taking cognizance of the manly self-image of his subjects.

Where the officer is not a "good cop," violence can be avoided if the officer is willing to enact fictions. If the suspect is allowed to demonstrate surface deference (sufficiently phoney to permit him to salvage his self-esteem) a peaceful resolution is possible. In the words of one delinquent,

If you kiss their a-- and say, "Yes Sir, No Sir," and all that jazz, then they'll let you go. If you don't say that, then they gonna take you in. And if you say it funny they gonna take you in. Like, "Yes, Sir! No Sir!" But if you stand up and say it straight, like "Yes Sir" and "No Sir" and all that, you cool [190, p. 87].

The Officer-Suspect Transaction

In police files, police violence is invariably assault on the police. But even as the police assault is officially described it is rarely a one-sided event. The most frequent motive for assaulting an officer that one finds in police reports is the suspect's indignation at having been tampered with on unconvincing grounds. In most such cases, the suspect serves notice of his resentment, but the officer perseveres in approaching him. Fully half of the violent police incidents reviewed in one study showed

the type of sequence where, in the first step, the officer starts an interaction with a civilian by means of an order, a demand, a suggestion, a question, a request, or some other communication. Usually, no serious offense has been committed by the civilian (where there is a formal infraction, the most common is a traffic violation) and the contact is classifiable either as preventive police work or as an effort to cope with a nuisance act. A group of boys is "told to move" or "questioned as to what they are doing"; an errant driver is "told to stop" or "notified" of his violation; a person who is engaged in an altercation is queried as to "what the problem was" or is "instructed to be quiet" or "told to go home." A request for name, address, or identification may also provide the opening spark of the sequence [178, p. 41].

An officer may claim that he is repeatedly assaulted because he is active and aggressively engaged in the pursuit of crime. Such a claim may be backed by good evidence, but gross indices of activity are apt to be deceptive, because they disguise qualitative differences. An officer can accumulate arrests by generating "on view" situations of questionable legality; he may exercise his discretion in a fundamentalist way by enforcing minor misdemeanors. Although productivity need not be achieved at the expense of quality, the combination of productivity and violence is suspect. This is particularly the case because police violence is usually associated with incidents that initially involve relatively minor infractions.

Our own work [178] suggests that chronically violent men—whether officers or civilians—contribute to their violence in a patterned way. They are not only involved often, but are also involved in similar ways on different occasions. This fact holds in situations where an aggressive man encounters a man who is not violently inclined, but also where two violent men interact. In such instances, each of the two parties tends to play an assigned role in his opponent's habitual game.

Even standard motives for police violence can reflect a recurrent theme, as the following interview excerpt illustrates:

I:[d] ... You say you don't like people pushing you around or that you hit this guy because he was pushing you around. You feel the same way about officers?

S: Yeah.

I: Did you feel the same way about these three guys that came along and hollered at you while you were walking with your girl?

S: Yeah. I felt the same.

I: Have you felt the same way in other fights you've had? That people were pushing you around and you got in a fight with them because you want to stop them pushing you?

S: Yeah [178, p. 121].

The individual quoted here is particularly instructive, because his incident with the police was typical of those discussed by Westley. The officer who was rebuffed by the man had then translated the man's protest into an image of mili-

---

[d] In these excerpts, "I" stands for the interviewer, and "S" for the officer or suspect being interviewed.

tant opposition to policing, and of attack on law and order. The officer tells the interviewer,

I feel that it couldn't be personal. The guy doesn't know me. Chances are very slim that I've ever seen him before. I probably don't know him from Adam, so I can't possibly feel that it's personal to me. It's directed at law and order, at . . . not justice. . . . things, today are growing so that the trend is, rather than correct a man when he's done something wrong, is to tell him that he's done something wrong, don't do it again. I can remember when I was a kid, if you talked to a police officer like I've been talked to, you would either wind up in the hospital or your folks would have you down in the jail and find out why. Now, I'm not saying that you should go out and beat up all the citizens, but I'm saying only that the respect for law enforcement is gone, not diminishing, it's gone. There is no respect for law enforcement at all [178, pp. 126–127].

Although a specially motivated officer has a higher probability than his peers to be involved in violence in any encounter, his chances are enhanced when he intercepts a violence-prone civilian. And meetings with violence-prone suspects become more probable when a policeman goes out of his way to arrange them, as in the case of an officer who interrupted a criminal interrogation to sermonize a group of swearing teenagers across the street, and provoked an incipient riot. This officer provides a good case for consistency, because on a second occasion he gratuitously intercepted a gang marching down a street. There ensued a tangential altercation with a female gang member who had decided to challenge the officer. He reacted to this challenge by invoking the law:

S: And she says, "F--k you, cop," and this was the straw that broke the camel's back.
I: Well, what do you think about when somebody says that?
S: You can't take it personally. This is something that—you know, I'm called so many names out there, and your own vocabulary is, turns into . . . you're a garbage mouth really because you're with it, you talk their language, and so, this doesn't bother me. But this was something—well, this was a personal affront to general law enforcement authority. I know this girl before. No respect for her parents, a pure incorrigible, and so this is the straw that broke the camel's back. She was going . . . [178, p. 117].

We discover the other side of the coin later, when the suspect (who is not noted for her even disposition) proceeds to wreck the officer's car:

S: . . . she's got the box (my report box) and has got a hold of that, and I'm trying to keep that down . . . she's throwing everything out of the box, the penal code, all my reports, there was maybe 400 pieces of paper and assignment cards, ticket book, everything went out of the car piece by piece. And she started to swear at this time, "I'm not going," and I was a great distance away from the car. . . .

I: You said she was getting mad here; she's not insane, she's mad?

S: She's been had [178, p. 119].

Preferred activity patterns of officers are related to their involvement in violence. A gruff officer is a problem, but a gruff officer who looks for action is a disaster. And not the least reason for concern is that such an officer, as he goes about his personal crusade, is apt to find targets in the shape of civilian counterparts. Once such a meeting occurs, the stage is set for the operationalizing of norms such as "respect."

Violent officers are visible in police records and responsible for much of police violence. They are also, however, systemic products. Although they court trouble, trouble is tied to productivity, which is esteemed. The act of violence itself ("interference" or "assault on a peace officer") thus turns into an arrest, which is a unit of police production.[e] And even where an officer's act is flagrant, it is still entitled—because it is police business—to protective measures.

It follows that the violence-prone officer cannot be dealt with as an individual problem. To target such an officer for attention calls into question organizational goals, such as wide discretion and high productivity. It also invites locker room resistance.

The locker room holds the premise that violence grows out of situational pressures, so that any officer is a potential candidate for transfer to Siberia. Even if the accusations are deemed meritorious (for instance, if Officer Smith is seen as a Dangerous Nut), there is always the concern with autonomy. If administrators can monkey with Smith—however unsavory he may be—they may be tempted to encroach on others.

The police assaulter is also immunized. For while the officer argues that he enforces law, the suspect claims that he is harassed by police. If the suspect's case is weak to start with, the borderline nature of his arrest gives it strength. A police assaulter cannot see a dispute as personal if it has been punished as a defiance of law, especially if the suspect equates the law with illegitimate police presence.

The difference between the officer and the assaulter is that the assaulter's subculture is not available to him where it counts. While the officer may obtain evasive testimony from his partner, the suspect's peers may make poor witnesses. The fact that a citizen does not have others rise to his defense may make him more vulnerable than the officer.

---

[e]Actually, this is true in a very narrow sense only. The San Francisco Police Department once found, for example, that fully half its interference and resistance arrests were dismissed, and an average of only 13 percent of arrestees were jailed [152].

Types of Police Violence

Putting aside the issue of change implications—to which we will return—what can we say so far? What is "police violence?" What defines it? Nurtures it? Gives it shape?

The literature, from Westley down, centers on police–citizen confrontations that end in assaults. It probably takes this turn because sheer prevalence permits inquiry yielding inferences backed by data. The strategy pays off nicely. The portrait traced by research holds over time, over place, over types of data. Observers, interviewers, incident analysts, converge on common substance.

Westley's view shows that violence, when used by police, responds often to taunts. It does so because the officer's self-love is gauged by "respect" from others. "Respect" for law, when a man feels he embodies law, inspires private wars under color of law. Few officers may be violent, but these are backed by others—by peers who see police bonds as links to survival.

We have filled in the details of this view. There is police socialization and the group's pull. Individual reactions to perceived affronts receive help from peer norms. Peer premises receive help from the job. All these merge in "police cynicism."

We have seen that violent suspects often tend to be counterparts of violent officers. These suspects also prize respect, and view it as a measure of self-esteem. This suggests that much police violence comes about when either party to a confrontation engages the other in a test of respect. Violence becomes probable where issues of self-esteem are mobilized for both contenders; it becomes less probable where one party retreats from the threat he poses to the other's self-esteem.

Although little is known about extreme police violence, we can assume that it is at least sometimes similar to the police violence familiar to us. This may hold particularly true in shootings that arise where relatively nonserious criminal charges are at issues (such as in domestic disturbances, investigations of suspicious persons, and traffic stops). Some such incidents may involve verbal interactions in which "affronted" individuals hold weapons, and in the heat of the moment come to deploy them.

It is also clear that the "cop and robber" game is sometimes at play. An officer faced with an on-view burglar is reluctant to let the suspect escape. Similarly, suspects faced with detention may take a short-range view of their fate, and attempt to shoot their way out. This may occur particularly in incidents where the suspect feels vulnerable, although the officer is unaware of the man's vulnerability.

There may also be suspects or officers disturbed enough to use weapons without realizing the full gravity of their acts. Guns are sufficiently available in our society, and sufficiently in use, for some persons to deploy them casually.

The presence of alcohol or strong feelings may create such casualness in individuals who are otherwise normal.

Finally, fear plays its role. This is particularly true where acts viewed through fear spawn "preventive" violence. The youngster who flees because police spell danger may be gunned down by an officer who feels threatened by the youngster's running. Such occasions are doubly tragic, because the two parties are victims of reciprocal errors.

It is worth repeating that violence arises out of violence and brings about more violence. A police obsessed with danger, a public in fear of police, produce polarization and distance. Fear increases in-grouping among police, which leads to isolation and cynicism, and breeds police violence.

3 Reducing Police Violence

Surveying violence reduction efforts in police departments is complicated by differences in the aim, philosophy, and rationale of programs and proposals. A police agency can think of itself as reducing violence by issuing hollow-point bullets, engaging in crisis intervention, screening recruits, tightening review procedures, clarifying rules, sponsoring sensitivity sessions, and reassigning personnel. In each case, the strategy may be based on different assumptions about the nature of violence, the aims of policing, and the process of change.

Screening Out and Weeding Out

Three decades ago, the psychoanalyst Paul Reiwald wrote that "a profession related to the enforcement of criminal justice, which makes use of force to such a degree, and moreover has need of it, attracts the aggressive elements in society, for it provides an excellent opportunity for exercising aggression" [146, p. 261].

Probably even today, the most popular assumption about police violence is that there are officers who are sadistic or violently prejudiced. Although police agencies do not share these assumptions, many departments seek to screen out violence-prone personalities among applicants through psychiatric interviews; if failures "sneak through" such screening, their supervisors are supposed to locate them subsequently. Thus, in the New York Police Department, "a list of 150 policemen who are considered by their superiors to be violence prone, extremely excitable, or unstable has been turned in to the police commissioner by precinct commanders throughout the city, as part of a new program to weed out policemen who are apt to use unnecessary violence in the performance of their duties" [109]. Although further developments with respect to this list were not publicized, the intent of the experiment was to put some men to pasture, and fire others. The commissioner described the program as unique, ("there is no other city in the country that's done it") but efforts to identify "violent officers" have been proposed elsewhere. For example, police psychiatrists are often invoked to test recruits for violence proneness. One psychiatrist, Dr. Martin Symonds, writes that "screening . . . is not sufficiently sensitive to detect a small percentage of men whose emotional problems will not be apparent until they undergo the unique stresses of police work, as well as the stresses produced by the nature of the department" [171, p. 6].

The information we have reviewed about police violence raises questions as to the efficacy of much of the current psychiatric screening of officers. If peer socialization, type of assignment, etc. have impact, the most important personal traits at issue may be a man's susceptibility to the locker room and to organizational pressures. It may be as important to determine whether a man has a strong need to gain peer approval as whether he has fondness for guns or blood-thirsty fantasies. Moreover, the interpersonal context of police violence suggests that screening must concentrate—more than it does—on situational tests featuring danger, challenges, and affronts. Such tests are available during the probationary period, if an agency avails itself of the opportunity to monitor each man's actions in a variety of supervised real-life encounters. Diagnostic field experiences (and simulated experiences) could be more generously employed, as they have been on occasion by the military [135].

To reduce peer support, carefully selected partners—enlightened and effective "old timers"—could add teeth to the recruit academy, so that what is tested is a man's disposition, rather than the peer group's influences working on him. The department that locates an overaggressive officer must then determine whether he can be resocialized, because it is not obvious that such a man must be discharged.

The practical problems in "weeding out" postprobationary officers—unless there are clear violations of rules—are substantial and serious. Beyond legal and civil rights problems, there are risks of lowering the morale and productivity of other men. These issues are raised both for reassignment and firing. They are raised for reassignment, because "insensitive" positions carry connotations of exile or prison. Daley recalls that

certain officers who had been judged somewhat unstable by the Police Medical Board were stripped of their guns, though not their shields, and assigned work as clerks or messenger boys, often in the basement offices at headquarters. This was known as the Rubber Gun Squad, or the Bow and Arrow Squad, and it was in many respects the ultimate disgrace that a policeman could experience [37, p. 31].

Reassignments and involuntary retirements spark predictable responses from police unions. If we are right in assuming that security concerns and "safety needs' are strong among criminal justice professionals, unilateral classification and assignment must be more threatening to officers than to workers in other organizations. There is also factual ambiguity in most street incidents, and officers feel strongly that their own versions of their encounters must be accepted. This has impact beyond morale; men operating under a system in which errors are penalized are liable to "play it safe" and underproduce.

Harding and Fahey [57] point out that police investigations of shootings in which "alternative credible versions" are offered, have rarely found officers liable. This historical backdrop creates expectations of immunity, which, when called into question, bring seemingly irrational reactions. This point holds for internal affairs investigations, external review proposals, and ombudsmen. Even the most scrupulous and conservative reviews, when newly institutionalized, evoke specters of arbitrariness. Officers do NOT feel entitled to unconditional immunity; they DO fear the precedents set by nonimmunity, with traditional safeguards removed.

The logic of violence control and the psychology of violence control are discrepant. Whereas the *logical* target of violence-reduction measures are men who are violent, the *psychological impact* of such measures is felt more often by men who are not. This phenomenon raises the strategic question of calculated risk: how strongly do we feel about bad apples to risk upsetting the barrel? The decision clearly cannot be lightly made.

Administrative Controls

The next most popular assumption about police violence is that if police officers are violent, their superiors must wish them to be violent. The rock bottom premise is that a police department that seriously objects to excessive force can curb abuses by its men administratively. All that is required is clear rules, serious supervision, and merciless discipline.

The shooting of civilians by police is sometimes seen as a reflection of organizational laxity. The "solution" is tighter rules governing the use of guns. Once a policy against shooting is on the books, there should be no shootings. Any residual problem becomes a matter of ambiguous guidelines, unsettled distinctions, and poor explication of rules. If the rules are clear, difficulties can only spell situations where officers defy or ignore rules. Such transgressions must invite disciplinary action.

The common law is generous toward police. It exonerates officers who kill suspects in order to accomplish clear felony arrests that cannot be consummated peacefully. The officer's own judgment here is generally taken at face value. The same holds in assessing the need for self-defense, where "the law does not require an officer to assume an unreasonable risk" [150, p. 752; also cf. 151, pp. 566 ff., and 161, pp. 132 ff.].

Although police agencies may not violate legal standards, they may *exceed* them; they may forbid an officer to shoot under circumstances in which the law does not. If the officer breaks such a rule without violating the law, he does not face prison, but may risk unemployment.

Administrative controls of this kind are favored by criminal justice professionals. The "Police" task force of the President's Commission on Law Enforcement [139] recommends "that all departments formulate written firearms policies which clearly limit (the use of firearms) to situations of strong and compelling need." The commission *specifically* adds that "a department should even place greater restrictions on their use than is legally required" [139, p. 189].

Surveys—some cited by the Crime Commission—reveal a picture short of the ideal. Many departments, including several in large cities, proved to have no written rules. Others had issued vague injunctions, prescribing "caution," "good judgment," and other nonoperationalizable standards. Diversity was extreme. A suspect able to safely flee from his crime could risk death by crossing a street or jumping a fence. The 1973 National Advisory Commission, in its police report, points out that

the potential consequences of the use of force demand that it be exercised with the greatest discretion; however, other than the broad language of the authorizing statutes and occasional imprecise court decisions, police officers receive little guidance regarding the manner or amount of the force they use [96, p. 18].

The issue of "guidance" mentioned by the commission is separable from that of "control." Control entails punishing those who have violated orders. Guidance means spelling out rules so as to make them clear, understandable, and translatable into action. A rule can be both informative and threatening, but need not be. An officer may be told to "use common sense" or risk early retirement. His "guidance" takes place after he has decided what "common sense" means to him. By then, it may be too late.

Guidelines may translate into training exercises involving group discussion, role playing, etc. Their context, in fact is *training,* and not (as with control) administration.

The emphasis matters. While "firearms regulations" as *controls* may deter, they invite predictable resistance. The risks assumed in such strategies are illustrated by a recent New York incident in which two officers who were acquitted of murdering a young boy were dismissed by their department. One of the officers was found guilty of shooting "wrongfully and without just cause"; the other was dismissed for lying to protect his partner. The *New York Times* reports that "the decision set off a wave of anger among policemen, who flooded the switchboard of the Patrolmen's Benevolent Association with calls voicing their outrage. . . . 'This is nothing but a case of bending to community and political pressure,' [the PBA Spokesman] said. 'Who do you turn to when the whole department is out to destroy you? Who can you turn to?'. . . He said he had four men manning the phones "to try to calm them down" [123].

The alternative—training—has risks too. Its premise—rationality—is not uniformly well-founded. Officers may be trigger-happy, or act out of fear. Such men profit minimally from information. Ex-commissioner Daley [37] notes that in training contexts officers who had shot people often "were listened to with awe by the others, principally because no one could know what it was like in combat except those who had been there" (p. 30). This fact qualifies training results, since it points to norms opposed to the aim of guidelines, even in the police academy itself.

Other limitations are intrinsic to training content. Thus, in New York City, firearms training is multidimensional. Ethics are stressed, as are strictures ("you may shoot only to defend yourself . . . "), techniques, and judgment. But training films contain incidents in which seemingly innocent interactions involve hidden threats. Such content cuts two ways. While it sensitizes men to danger, the lesson of danger may be too well or too indiscriminately absorbed. Where danger cues are ambiguous, caution may be hard to distinguish from panic. In a recent incident in New York, a patrolman who killed a boy armed with a tool testified that:

What my eyes saw for a gun was pointed directly at my chest. . . . There was no time to disarm him. I could only fire my gun and protect my life. I couldn't wait a second or two. I was dead. I didn't fire loosely. I fired when I was going to die. . . . I didn't shoot anybody in cold blood. . . . I shot him down because I was going to die. I felt it was either my life or his [129].

Although training may attempt to teach *discrimination* of danger it is not clear whether hidden messages (such as "death finds you where you least expect it") are not dominant for some trainees.

Violence control measures run into special difficulties because they challenge the "warfare model" of the Crimefighting Officer. A PBA spokesman told the *New York Times* that "cops are basically afraid to do the job—they're afraid to use their weapon, and afraid to act without it. There's a general paranoia that hampers the cops. . . . It's not a police department any more. We're a social agency. 'With the rate of civilian shootings of police going down, the rate of crime is going up. . . . You have to relate the two'" [130].

Control is not the issue here. The real concern is with the definition of the police mission, and with its priorities. Where the contention is that officers are "afraid to do *the* job," that theirs is "not a police department any more," and that they are "hampered," one defines the context of shootings. With crime-fighting-no-holds-barred, lives must be taken. To restrict force implies that crime-fighting ends are sacrificed.

Firearms rules trade crimes for lives. Fleet-footed burglars may flee, and hot cars escape. Full enforcement is clearly short-changed for due process [194]. Ethnic polarization is avoided, which fuels charges that "community pressure groups" are "catered to." The police mission is *in fact* redirected toward broader goals than those envisaged by some (or most) officers.

Detroit's STRESS unit helps make this point. Suspects did attack the unit's decoys, and "good arrests" were made. The issue became one of maintaining a "crime-fighting" unit at increased expense in lives. Files of the New York

Police Department show disproportionate shooting done by operations such as "stake-out" squads.[a] Such groups are tight, high-morale subcultures, which are geared to combat. Firearm rules, to such groups, imply serious compromise with strongly felt aims.

Whether the emphasis is on control or training, violence-reduction efforts must note their corollaries. To stress both violence reduction *and* crime fighting produces conflict and tension. The officer who is instructed to maximize his arrests and minimize his violence receives the sort of double message we have discussed. Firearms restrictions imposed on legalistic departments´ are transplants, and they produce systemic efforts at rejection. I propose to argue (in chapter 8) that violence reduction implies a more balanced view of the criminal-justice mission, which must be conveyed hand-in-hand with violence-related rules.

To illustrate alternate possibilities for administrative emphasis by police, a model is furnished by the ABA Manual on Police Standards [1], which recommends that

among other things, police effectiveness should be measured in accordance with the extent to which they:
(i) safeguard freedom, preserve life and property, protect the constitutional rights of citizens and maintain respect for the rule of law by proper enforcement thereof, and preserve democratic government;
(ii) develop a reputation for fairness, civility, and integrity that wins the respect of all citizens, including minority or disadvantaged groups;
(iii) use the minimum amount of force reasonably necessary in responding to any given situation;
(iv) conform to rules of law and administrative rules and procedures particularly those which specify proper standards of behavior in dealing with citizens;
(v) resolve individual and group conflict; and
(vi) refer those in need to community resources· that have the capacity to provide needed assistance.

The ABA suggests that:

Traditional criteria such as the number of arrests that are made are inappropriate measures of the quality of performance of individual officers. Instead, police officers should be rewarded, in terms of status, compensation, and promotion, on the basis of criteria defined in this section which directly relate to the objectives, priorities, and essential principles of police services. (p. 19)

Standards such as these (beyond what intrinsic merit they have) show administrators how to mitigate the control aspects of restrictions. By rewarding positive conduct, they permit the aims of change to take hold. They also make

---

[a]Such units may also be more lethal. A formal New York City Stakeout Squad, in 47 instances of firearm use, fired 128 shots, of which 100 proved hits. In these incidents, 21 suspects were killed, and 20 injured.

training consonant with the "reality" of prized ends. The first point is crucial. Punishing an officer who shoots a burglar, while rewarding his partner who makes a "hot arrest" and starts a riot, is in fact arbitrary. It increases the desire to "earn" arrests *at any price,* while making the price sometimes too high. Fear and reward run hand-in-hand, calling for hard discriminations. The control of zeal seems dictated by whim. But if due process solutions of crime problems are rewarded, violence infractions become deviations from operationalized goals. A man is punished because he has interfered with system ends, not because he has pursued them diligently, but unwisely. The controls are more congruent with the mission.

Police-Community Relations

If we contacted any police expert three decades back, he would prescribe "reducing prejudice" as his answer to violence.[b] For police, the experts wanted "special training in minority problems," as fleshed out by Lohman [77]. Such training included sections on "the role, of the police officer in dealing with tension." It stressed *facts* about race or culture, to make officers "objective" about citizens who were dissimilar to them.

The special training movement gained potency from the "zoot-suit" riots and similar confrontations of 1943. It was helped by critics who blamed such events on police, or who unfavorably characterized the enforcement responses to rioters [24].

However, "reducing prejudice" was seen to cut two ways; citizens must be "objective" about police—hence, favorably disposed toward police. This sometimes entailed the creation of "police-community relations (PCR)" units, whose job it was to reduce hostility to policing. The activities of the police departments, and the PCR units, varied. One of three concerns—as listed by Radelet [140, pp. 27-28] was "public relations." This function, which involved presenting a good police image to citizens, comprised such items as institutionalized courtesy, blazers, speakers, open houses, dog shows, bumper stickers, and awards to citizens. A related function was "community service," which covered outreach efforts by officers. Such efforts included police athletic leagues, officer friendlies, safety education, ride-ins, drum-and-bugle corps, tire changing, counselling, crisis intervention, ambulances, and house checks.

---

[b]The presumption that prejudice leads to police violence has raised questions. Experts today (including the President's Crime Commission) believe that officers' "private" attitudes can be held in check by a professional stance toward their work. Albert Reiss has documented this conclusion through an observational study, which showed that "although more than three-fourths of all white officers made prejudiced statements about Negroes, in actual encounters the police did not treat Negroes uncivilly more often than they did whites. . . . Whether police use excessive force depends more upon conditions of the encounter than on racial prejudice" [145, p. 147].

These types of programs were designed to interface the public with officers in constructive nonadversary roles.

Other programs involved "community participation." This type of effort stressed *joint activities* by officers and citizens in various sorts of community groups, particularly those concerned with community relations and tension reduction.

Police units concerned with public relations, community service, and community participation have lost their prominence and appeal. The stress, today, is on PCR *as a component of everything the police does.* Radelet [140] notes that

> properly understood, the principle is one for total *orientation* of a police organization. It is an attitude and an emphasis for all phases of police work, not merely for a specialized unit in the department.... Every problem in police work today is in some way a problem of police–community relations. Its solution depends in some sense upon police and community cooperation, indeed partnership. (p. 24)

The decline of PCRUs occurred because such units were of questionable effectiveness, and stood out like sore thumbs in enforcement-centered agencies. If PCRU members took their jobs lightly, they were pitied as exiles. If they took themselves seriously, they risked contempt by their peers. Other officers were not at all affected by PCRUs. The community impact was largely on middle-class publics who already favored the police.

With "department-wide community relations" the emphasis turned to training. But where the impact of community-relations training was evaluated, officer attitudes often seemed unaffected [140, p. 545]. Some innovations ("sensitivity exercises," "confrontation sessions," etc.) were frequently resented; human relations lectures tended to be seen as superfluous and as patronizing. Men emerged from classrooms with clenched teeth, and—at best—bored. "O.D." Laboratory sessions for senior personnel tended to offer more positive experiences, but the carryover was problematic. Even where participants were street personnel (which was rarely the case) they soon discovered the unbridgeable distance from "The Group" to life. Minisubcultures lasted through the group meeting, past the coffee hour, to casual encounters with fellow sectarians. But the police subculture tended to neutralize the warm glow of the miniculture. As long as wider subcultural forces exerted their impact, the convert's hope of influencing his own organization had all the potency of Custer's Last Stand.

Peer Review Panels

A special training venture that has encountered none of the usual resistances is a patrolman-run "peer review panel" developed in Oakland, California. This program is partly successful because it was designed by active policemen and street officers.[c] Other reasons for the appeal of the program lie in some of its content or structural features. For instance,

1. Panel staff are usually *peers* of panel subjects. Most of the staff are active on the streets; many are prestige figures; many have violence histories. There are always some men who have worked closely with the trainee.

2. Panel subjects are selected in terms of their *conduct.* Although some are referred by superiors (or self-referred), most exceed a predefined maximum number of violent incidents with citizens during a given period. The panel reviews *all* arrest reports in its police department, and keeps tallies of deployed violence. Subjects are seen after the panel has reviewed their reports, and has dissected out any special patterns of behavior it can find.

3. The review panel's function is to help a subject understand his own conduct, and to provide an atmosphere in which he can evolve alternative approaches. The panel views its role as supportive and educative. It strives for rapport, but uses peer pressure in modulated ways. Where the initial panel has little impact, a second panel may escalate the group's pressure.

4. Panels focus on concrete incidents as these emerge in the subject's reports, and in his responses to questioning. The panel centers on commonalities in the incidents, and on the man's behavioral contributions to violence. It explores concrete alternatives to the patterns it isolates.

5. Panel proceedings are confidential, and information about their substance is confined to panel members. In addition to being assured of confidentiality, the panel subjects know that no consequences can accrue from panel reviews. Officers are never seen while cases are pending in disciplinary proceedings; the emphasis is on *preventing the contingency of discipline.*

6. Panel subjects are the objects of continuing review. If new involvement in violent incidents is observed, there are follow-up interventions. But if the incidents decrease, as they tend to, the subject becomes a participant in future panels.

7. The panel engages in efforts to generate understanding of its work at all levels of the police organization. By rotating most of the panel membership (while maintaining continuity) an increasing number of men gain first-hand experience with the panel, and they serve as information sources among peers.

The success of the panel experiment is documented by recidivism statistics [179]. Throughout the panel's lifetime—which now spans five years—the group has contributed to overall reductions in numbers of violent incidents and

---

[c]The story behind the genesis of the panel is reported in detail by Toch, Grant, and Galvin [179]. The panel has spread from Oakland to other police departments, most notably to the Kansas City Police Department.

citizen complaints. Most panel subjects have dropped from extreme violence chronicity to moderate involvement or noninvolvement in violence. Retrospective interviews suggest that panel subjects feel themselves positively benefited. Many have become strong advocates of the procedure in their locker room.

The peer panel may owe its success mostly to the fact that it provides a vehicle for the police culture to influence its deviant members, without violating taboos of in-group loyalty. The panel harnesses solidarity in support of norms, which are even more supportive than those that protect a peer *despite* his conduct, or that publicly suppress information that is known throughout the organization. The procedure brings the administration and the ranks together, because no one wants to fire a cop. Internal reviews, from "whitewash" to "hard-nosed," are troublesome to the reviewers and to those reviewed. As an alternative, the panel reduces the need for administrators to incur the wrath of subordinates. The panel is also based on a fairly realistic definition of its target. We have seen that violent officers are neither completely different from their peers, nor representative of them; but they are often targeted as one or the other. The panel views its subject as "normal," but as reacting badly in *some* situations. This view coincides with the data, and addresses a portrait recognized as plausible by its subject and by his peers.

The panel is also designed to be minimally divisive. Since it assumes that its subjects are persons of integrity (and intelligence) it does not insult them, stigmatize them, or cause them shame. It does not mobilize the protective loyalty of their friends. Ultimately involving the subject as panelist, the program also removes the stigma of their subject status.

A final benefit relates to spread-of-effect. Antiviolence norms are carried from panels through the locker room by means of informal channels of influence. Over time, more officers with first-hand experience become carriers of the norms. In this fashion, "minipanels" are generated in police cars, which, ultimately, may supplant the more artificial intervention of the panel itself.

Violence Reduction Through Organizational Change

Oakland's panel enjoyed the support of its department. This support not only included resources, but also the climate of a due-process orientation. At the time of the panel's birth, Oakland had undergone a philosophical shift, which included deemphasis of whole-hog crime fighting, and stress on expanded service. If the clock were to turn back, the panel (and parallel interventions) might be hard put to survive. The reason for this is that police violence is linked to other aspects of policing. If officers confine themselves to helping old ladies, occasions for violence seldom arise. But violence is promoted if police aggressively round up belligerent drunks, arrest domestic disputants at the first whiff of a complaint, and chase teenagers off street corners whenever they can. "Search and destroy" lineup talks and a "no-questions-asked" style of supervision can also raise incentives for violence.

It thus seems that (1) overall police policies or programs can impede or facilitate violence; (2) violence is never reduced if enforcement goals that encourage violence are stipulated; (3) programs that are aimed at changing police goals are likely to have impact on violence levels, and (4) where police violence is reduced, we can expect change in the remainder of the department.

All sorts of police reforms can reduce violence while really having other purposes in mind. Cases in point include experiments such as team policing, crisis intervention units, and policewomen on patrol. Team policing is the purest example of structural reorganization. It delegates to an informally organized "team" of officers the responsibility for policing its neighborhood. In theory, the police are brought closer to the community, they can adjust their activities to community needs, and can work closely with citizen representatives. If this principle held, the violence-reduction potential would be obvious: teenage gang members are not likely to play "wise-guy" roles with a man in a yellow blazer who coaches their softball team; riots do not form among spectators to an arrest that is inspired by a community plea voiced in church two nights previously.

The theory, however, can boomerang. A police team may avail itself of its freedom to set up a "wild-west" model of enforcement, complete with round-ups of "bad eggs," harassment, and sundowning. Segments of the community may exert pressure towards summary enforcement. As noted by Sherman *et al.* [157] ,

The community may make strong demands for the police to be "tough guys" in order to clean up crime, in ways that, if not illegal, are in contradiction to the model conceived by police administrators. For example, data from the evaluation of the New York City program shows that some teams increased the use of aggressive tactics, specifically illegal stop and frisks. Early data from the Cincinnati evaluation tentatively suggests the same trend. (p. 108).

In theory, the police team can create a subculture of its own. While the headquarters patrol force may persist in its admiration of men who splinter batons on skulls, the "heroes of the store front" can be masters of blarney or pied pipers for neighborhood youth. Moreover, a team (unlike the main force) may use civilians as arbiters of their self-esteem. An officer may come to gauge his worth by the number of residents who joyfully greet him (on a first-name basis) as he walks or drives by. Such links can dilute the hold of the headquarters locker room over team members, and can decrease the subcultural solidarity of the store front itself.

The problem with such developments lies in the backlash they produce. Competitions ensue, and administrators worry about the control they exercise.

Police departments see themselves giving birth to "minidepartments" that make their own policies, drain resources, and engage in rivalry with the main force. The "model precinct" becomes the "problem precinct." Instead of spread-of-effect from the team to the department, pressures arise in the department to reintegrate the experiment.

Family Crisis Intervention

Like team policing, family-crisis management is an activity with violence impact. Although officers hold family fight calls in low esteem,[d] a large proportion of dispatched police contacts involve domestic disturbances; officers *must* respond to these calls. The closest they can come to avoiding them is to terminate each mandated contact as quickly as possible.

Morton Bard's well-known Family Crisis Intervention (FCI) experiment makes the resolution of family fights a skilled and prized activity for trained patrolmen. Although the men in Bard's experiment continued to exercise general police functions, they acquired special skills for handling family conflicts. Their impact on violence was very direct [7, 8].

Family fights are a disproportionate source of police injuries. Skilled officers can escape violence produced by mis-cued responses. Moreover, with a family's problems "solved," police contacts, with their attendant risks of injury, should recur less often. (The first assumption appears to hold; however, satisfied clients of family crisis teams have shown a tendency to call for future police services.)

A more direct impact of the FCI program relates to a change in the officers' outlook. As Bard put the matter,

It has been possible to deal with the "masculine mystique" which has helped make police so malleable at the hands of those who have been interested in provoking violence. Group pressures and sanctions have served to afford recognition to the skillful and effective officer who can "cool" a situation to the point where the disputants can begin to communicate with each other. The men were encouraged to develop their own style for restructuring the initial perceptions of the disruptants toward police. The response repertoire of the officers has been expanded, and their sense of mastery enhanced [7, p. 53].

The change that is described by Bard is not one of personal orientation. It is a shift in the conception of police activity. Bard advocates a "generalist

---

[d]Symptomatic of the view is the following *New York Times* item [107], which originates in a model New York precinct, and therefore is a mild version of the attitude: "Sometimes the police make small jokes about it. Radio cars pull up alongside one another, policemen lean out the window, and one says gravely to the other: "I have just adjudicated another situation."

specialist" model, which keeps men doing patrol work; the prescription makes it less likely that FCI unit members be labeled "social workers in uniform," and ostracized by their peers.

Within limits, this principle seems to work, but the "specialist" feature tends to intrude. The esprit de corps of FCI officers, which is based on shared experiences and new professionalism, is very high. The men can become an elite enclave or group. Spread-of-effect from such a group to the rest of the police force is likely to be minimal. Training manuals and referral agency lists cannot bridge the conceptual gap between sophisticated specialists and their peers.

Women on Patrol

Policewomen have entered patrolwork through affirmative action trends in the nonpolice world. The development has been bolstered by courts and legislation, and has been strongly resisted by police unions, police wives, and many rank and file officers. The violence theme has often been cited in arguments against using policewomen in patrol work, with the principal issue revolving around the chances of an officer having to fight on his beat. The opposition to patrol-women implies that physical conflicts are prevalent. This presumption is an article of faith with critics, since statistics seem not to phaze them. The *New York Times,* in describing precinct "rap sessions" by New York Commissioner Cawley, quotes the following dialogue:

Officer Mugan: "But it's a built-in feeling to protect a female. If they are considered equal how come in the Olympics they didn't have females competing against the men, say in weightlifting, the 100-yard dash, boxing and wrestling. They can't do it. They could not compete."
Commissioner Cawley: "I'm not saying they can compete on a physical scale in all situations. But let me give you another standard. Our statistics show that 90 percent of the normal function of a police officer involves providing service; 2 percent involves some physical activity." Officer Mugan accepts the statement but seems unconvinced [116].

Male patrolmen must often satisfy minimal height requirements for police candidacy. Such requirements are based on the same violence premise—that police work entails the need for a good deal of physical combat. If the physical fitness requirement is applied to women, it can be dismissed by the courts as a discriminatory procedure. The height requirement, however, can be viewed as an "objective" index, which happens to eliminate all but jolly female giants by reason of height rather than gender. If short people are unqualified for police work, it is viewed as irrelevant that most women (or Latin men) are physically excluded.

To defend the height requirement, the violence argument is buttressed by data purporting to show higher assault rates for shorter men. The difficulites are that the height differences, where found, are minor and that all the statistics pertain to men. This last fact is crucial because the finding is subject to a very different interpretation from the one conventionally suggested. If shorter officers are assaulted more frequently, the safest assumption (in terms of what we know about the "shape of police violence") is that they are more likely to start a fight, rather than that they cannot handle its consequences. This view is supported by the finding of some studies [e.g., 59], that height is correlated with civilian complaints.

We may assume that *at least some* smaller officers must be cognizant of the importance that is assigned to physical stature in the working-class male world and in the police male world. This awareness might lead unself-assured individuals to overreact to situations in which a personal challenge—a test of their competence—is perceived. As diagnosed by the mayor of Albany, New York, "A little short fella, he's more aggressive. He compensates for the lack of stature with aggressive behavior" [174].

The plausibility of explanations centered on self-esteem and social inter-action is crucial, because it *is* sex-linked. It remains a peculiarly male (and predominantly working-class male) value to emphasize physical prowess as a criterion of worth. And this value is sharpened by the police culture, with its emphasis on danger and physical involvement on the street. The argument be-comes self-fulfilling. It *begins* with the assumption that combat potential is crucial; it pounds this assumption into the minds of men who are most likely to feel inferior as a result, and it *ends* by deducing a man's inadequacy from his efforts to prove himself by living up to the myth.

The presumption is plausible that women, who are not likely to share the valuation of physical power, might be less likely than *any* male patrolman—tall or short—to test their adequacy by participating in violence. The arguments for early experiments with female patrolmen appear to imply this hypothesis [90].

It would follow that if female officers resist becoming minimale amazons (and playing roles similar to those of the overcompensating "small officer") they can contribute to a more balanced view of policing. This may entail more specialized use of women on patrol than some police agencies, experts, and feminists may care for. It could involve at first using women for human service functions to help develop these functions through effective performance. Such a move may provide a wedge for the undermining of the artificial combat model that enthralls police agencies, despite the fact that the bulk of police activities take place in the service realm, and are sometimes immensely well discharged.[e]

---

[e]Police effectiveness in peacekeeping roles generally [36], in approaches to the mentally ill [13], in the handling of skid-row cases [14], shows that male officers can perform exceedingly well in the service realm.

For a policewoman to have impact, the integrity of her sex role—with its deemphasis of physical prowess and combativeness as indexes of status—is a critical variable. The police culture is male. It is, in fact, *super*-male: it forces some men, some of the time, to posture exaggerated male traits. The strain is present for men, but the incongruity, if women emulated caricatures of male conduct, could be serious. Demonstrations of toughness—which are easier than many men pretend—do not bring into play the interpersonal strengths that women (and men) potentially possess, and that the police desperately need. To be effective police officers, women must be permitted to excel in ways that can modulate the male emphasis of the locker room.[f]

This task is hard. Patrolwomen are "marginal," in the sense of aspiring to acceptance by patrolmen.[g] In similar contexts, people adopt norms that are calculated to gain them in-group acceptance. They can also play special roles (such as that of weak sister) that are acceptable but stultifying.[h] The challenge to policewomen is to resist male pressures, and to develop identities that help round out the police in violence-reducing ways.

Beyond Crime Fighting

Organizational change that "rounds out" policing need not short-change crime fighting. Felony arrests rank as key police acts; there *are* armed suspects who shoot, and who must (sometimes) be shot. Police agencies must deal effectively with crime-related functions, including those calling for force.

Danger is a fact of police life. Just as no pilot can abrogate concern for safety rules, the policeman must stand ready to meet danger. By the same token, the man obsessed with danger can become (where there is no danger) a boor. The airline pilot's intercom messages would sound odd if they reflected the stance of the Red Baron, or that of a man perpetually worried about the adequacy of his fuel supply. The pilot has (in the shape of passengers) a peacekeeping role. By observing safety rules, he preserves others from death or injury.

In policing, the problem with danger and combat is that the stress may

---

[f]The final report of the "Policewomen on Patrol" study [16] contains illustrative incidents of policewomen's interventions in domestic (and other) disturbances. The quality of the interventions ranges from innocuous to clumsy, and suggests a need for special training to help women deploy their skill in crisis management.

[g]The concept of "marginality" was first developed by Kurt Lewin [73]. It describes a person "who stands on the boundary . . . between two groups. . . . He does not belong to either of them, or at least he is not certain about his belongingness." The most common observation about marginality (as summarized by Krech and Crutchfield [72] is that "the marginal man reacts by overemphasizing conformity to the cultural pattern of the group with which he wishes to establish strong identification" (p. 488).

[h]Initial surveys show a tendency for patrolwomen to permit their partners to "take over" [16].

bridge to where no danger exists and where combat is a silly option. For some officers, fear is an issue because they are unsure of themselves. Every officer must face fear. It affects his perspective [160], although the locker room makes it unfashionable to surface this fact. Covert fear, however, distorts perception by inventing threats; it may produce overreactions and bravado [69] and may provoke suspects to overreact in their turn. When officers rush in to rescue a fear-obsessed peer, they often meet violence that should never have occurred.

The virtue of an emphasis on positive police functions lies in its potential for reducing the obsession with control aspects of policing. To achieve this end, service modalities must help define and round out police aims [91]. A compartmentalized positive function can help increase a department's capabilities for delivery of services, but it loses the benefits of the strategy to the organization itself. The danger can be remedied by integrating positive functions in the organization. One can forge links between police teams and headquarters; FCI officers may be involved in training other men, and by being used throughout the patrol force; police women may be placed so as to help model a nonmacho approach to police work.

As we shall show in chapter 8, such developments have wider systemic impact than we suspect. Police agencies can gain staff development and enhance citizen suppport. They can lessen the strain they now face in training men, and in explaining their jobs to them. There would be less need for admiring work that occurs infrequently, that is dangerous and adversary, and invokes few skills. And as men learn to prize what they do, they should be less obsessed with what they do not do—such as fight, conquer, survive, or perish.

4 The Shape of Prison Violence

The man in the street expects prisons to control people. He sees walls and towers; he knows that inmates spend time in cells, with much surveillance. He assumes trouble can be curtailed by supervision.

But the man in the street does expect trouble in prisons. He knows that prisons house felons, who are thrown together and detained by force. Prisons make news through riots. Books and films on prisons highlight brutal acts. In documentaries, the viewer sees makeshift weapons where cells are searched. He reads of inmate "militance." Most felons, he hears, are revolutionaries. Others rape peers. Gangs and syndicates move behind walls; they make war, spread terror. Guards beat inmates.

What are the Facts?

The man on the street is right on one count. He—the "average person"—would be safer on the street than in prison. But inmates are not "average"; they incur more risk, when free, than other men.

We know that few inmates are killed in prisons. In 1964 and 1965, the number of prisoner homicide victims for the entire country averaged 40 men [155]. A recent estimate [197] placed the annual total at 120 to 130. Ironically, in the same recent year (1973), 100 students were murdered in schools included in a selective, incomplete survey [12].

Fast custodial response and good surgery save lives. For every stabbed inmate who does not survive, nine others do survive. Prison assault rates are probably no higher than the rates for slum taverns, street corners, and homes.

None of this is really consoling. For one, there are jails and prisons that are *very* dangerous. In Philadelphia, estimates had it that 1 out of 30 jail inmates was forcibly raped [39]. In one year (1974), 13 men died in San Quentin; the previous year, prison inmates executed each other in large numbers at Walpole in Massachusetts. Violence rates in most prisons are increasing much faster than those in free society. In 1970, a California inmate had one chance in a hundred of being seriously hurt; his chances had increased four-fold by 1974.

Jails and prisons, moreover, have a climate of violence that has no free world counterpart.[a] Inmates are terrorized by other inmates, and spend years in

---

[a]The President's Crime Commission tells us that "a prisoner's prime concern in a traditional institution is to cope with the most aggressive inmates. He comes to have an extreme dis-

47

fear of harm. Some inmates request segregation, others lock themselves in, and some are hermits by choice. Many inmates injure themselves.

The "testing out" of new arrivals by their peers leaves many a first offender feeling vulnerable. Rumors of danger are rife. In jails, inmates who have already spent time in the "pen" or who claim to know what happens there spread horrifying tales about brutality. Recipients of such accounts arrive in prison expecting to struggle for their survival. Such fears cause problems beyond the immediately obvious ones. In prison, fear is a stigma of weakness, and it marks men as fair game for exploitation. And staff attention to an inmate who fears for his safety can label him a "snitch" and make him doubly vulnerable [65]. Inmate norms contain implicit threats of violence. Unpaid debts call for use of force; group loyalties prescribe retaliation for slights to group members. There is also the norm of "fight of flight": beleaguered inmates are told (by both fellow inmates and staff) to do battle unless they wish to seek refuge in segregation.

The most surprising feature of prison is that—except for riots—staff–inmate violence is minimal. This is especially striking because the power of staff is mostly illusory [170]. Men in prisons have little to lose. Guards are outnumbered. Punishment may confer prestige to the punished. And inmates hate guards.

Yet, despite recent increases in violent incidents there are few inmates who assault staff; individual custodial attacks on inmates are also—despite prison folklore—few. Overt violence in prison is mostly confined to inmate attacks on inmates, or on themselves.

Inmate Assaults

Except for a survey on North Carolina [44], empirical data on inmate assaults are derived mainly from research by California penologists. This limits the value of the data, since California may be different from other states. In some ways, though, there are compensations. We have a portrait of violence in one state prison system over time; we see the trends and the subtrends.

There are trends that simply reflect our changing perceptions of the violence problem. Research has moved from efforts to describe "violent persons" through a view of "incidents," to a concern with groups or gangs. Early researchers sought explanations for violence in the personal histories of inmates; they saw derivatives of broken homes, with histories of neglect and odd psychological test profiles [64]. Later research noted prison-specific violence that was often repeated [94]. Currently, the view centers on inmate groups that favor violence to support antisocial group ends [169].

But we have facts that are constants. Prison violence is centered, in every

trust of all persons, but especially of the officials. *He sees violence or threat of violence as a practical necessity for preserving self-integrity in even relatively minor conflict situations"* [138, p. 47; italics added].

period surveyed, among street youths, and it links some to past violence. To understand the causes of violence we must understand the impact of both these constants, and of other, more variable forces. We must first view population trends, for where our prisons house different men, we expect different patterns of inmate conduct.

In California, the effects of "decarceration" are clearly manifest over time. Men who were formerly sent to prison are now returned to counties, for "community" treatment. In 1960, 28 percent of those who were convicted of felonies in California were committed to prison by the Corrections Department; by 1970, the proportion of convicted felons who were incarcerated had decreased to 10 percent of those convicted. This decrease did not take place across the board. Although all categories of offenses showed decreases, some showed larger decrements than others. A man found guilty of willful murder had an 80 percent chance of imprisonment in 1960, and a 60 percent chance in 1972. Robbers stood a 60 percent risk of prison in 1960, but only a 33 percent risk in 1972. One burglar and check forger out of three went to prison in 1960; by 1972, only one out of ten was confined.

As a consequence of such changes, the California prison population became not only more select, but quite different. Homicide and robbery offenders accounted for 17 percent of the 1960 prison census; by 1972, *one out of three* prisoners stood convicted of one or the other offense. On the other hand, burglary and forgery suspects had dropped from 40 percent to 20 percent of the prison population. These changes obscure other facts. In most offense categories, the 1972 prisoners were a different breed. Four out of five forgers in California prisons as of 1960 had records free of violence; by 1972, the proportion of forgers with violent pasts had reached 50 percent. Where most homicide inmates in 1960 had no prior violence involvements, the killers of 1972 tended to have past experience with violence.

These changes gain significance as we review information about the men responsible for violent incidents. A 1964 California task force found that one out of ten of the prison aggressors had been convicted of assault on the street; by 1973, the proportion had risen from 10 percent to 15 percent. In the same interval the proportion of men convicted of assault in the prison population had increased from 4.5 percent to 7.4 percent. This means that the number of prison aggressors who had been assaultive in the streets stood constant at twice the "expected" number. The issue with respect to homicide is more complex: In 1963, 8.4 percent of the prison population had been convicted of homicide, and the prison aggressor group included 8 percent homicide offenders, which is precisely the same proportion as in population. By 1973, 15 percent of California prison inmates stood convicted of murder. Among prison aggressors, however, the proportion of convicted murderers had increased to 24 percent, which is a real disproportion. On the other hand, we have noted that the murderer of 1973 was probably a generally different offender—a man prone to repeated violence.

There are trends in California that are much more surprising. In California prisons, Mexican-Americans make up a stable 18 percent of the inmate body. The proportion of prison aggressors who are Latin, however, increased from 26 percent in 1963, which is high, to 40 percent in 1973, which is astronomical. The issue of age is more constant. In 1963, the 20-24 age group made up 19 percent of the adult inmate population; in 1973, the cohort was 22 percent of the total. This age group is disproportionately violent, but the disproportion varies; men 20-24 constituted 43 percent of the aggressor group in 1963; ten years later, the number ranged from 30 percent to 55 percent of prison aggressors.

Interpretation of such facts is not a simple matter. Age is linked to the perpetration of violence not only in prisons, but generally. Young men are responsible for most of the assaults we witness in the streets, in schools, and elsewhere. Many of the forces that spawn violence among young inmates may be no different than the forces that have inspired and increased violence among young males generally. The impact of ethnicity is also related to what happens outside prison. Violence in San Quentin and Soledad may derive from forces at work in Mexican street gangs in Los Angeles and Bakersfield; violence in New York prisons may mirror the ghetto norms of Harlem. All prisons must inherit their subcultural sediments from the street corners that supply them with clients.

In assessing the role of demographic factors, three facts are important: First, even where a factor is associated with *most* prison incidents, it can only account for some of the people who fit the general description that is involved. If 2 percent to 4 percent of all inmates participate in assaults, aggressors must be minority of *any* standard inmate group. If half the prison aggressors in California are Mexican-Americans, which they were for a few months in 1973, this total comprises one of ten Latin inmates; it tells us little about the other nine Mexican-American inmates. It is possible—in fact, plausible—that most Mexican prison aggressors are loyal clique members, and that many of their compatriots are not.

This consideration relates to another, which is that factors combine—inextricably—in people. An inmate may be a young Mexican-American street gang member with an extensive history of assaults. He is other things, too. He is a summary of traits, only some of which we can count. The man's presence in inventories of aggressive youths, Latins, clique members, or orphans describes correlates of his violence without assigning priorities to variables. The critical factor might be the man's "macho" values and the congruent norms of the prison yard.

Moreover, the picture we have traced is of *conjoint* population shifts. Groups combine people. Decarceration has filled the prison yard more homogeneously with tough inmates. This may mean that men who were stabilizing forces have been decarcerated, and that prisons are now filled with men who grate more menacingly on each other. It may mean that cliques have sprung up as prison yards have come to more closely resemble the streets.

It is clear that when prisons throw tough men together—if other things stay constant—they reap inmate assaults. Disciplinary segregation settings show disproportionate violence, and if they are very generously used (as in 1974 in California), they run out of control.[b]

The Occasion for Assault

We do not know how much prison violence in 1985 will consist of clique-related revenge, or will relate to ethnicity or past violence. We do know that as long as there are prisons, there are situational causes of violence that will always remain with us. This is so, because such occasions for violence are built into the circumstances of prison life, and into the values engendered by prisons.

Summaries of typical California incidents, culled from forms submitted in the early sixties, permit a survey of routine motives for institutional assaults. They make it clear that prison homosexuality often leads to prison violence.[c] Homosexually inspired violence in prison may sometimes take forms similar to heterosexual violence elsewhere, as in refusals to accept the end of a relationship, or in issues of rejection and pride:

A "close relationship" has been known to exist between B and K, who have on several occasions been discovered in compromising and unseemly positions. Their relationship, however, appears to be disintegrating. In the incident, K wants to talk to B, who doesn't want to talk to K. K tries to take B to the yard for a conversation, and a fight ensues.[d]

Less analogous to street violence are the less frequent incidents associated with the use of force to secure sexual submission. Although rape (or gang rape) may be replicated in back alleys or parking lots, the converse—violence in defense of sexual integrity—is more prison-specific. We have noted that prison and jail norms call for demonstrations of pugnaciousness as countermeasures to pressure. Some inmates, out of fear, may deploy the strategy prematurely, or more

---

[b]In 1963, few California inmates (1.5% of population) were confined in segregation, but 17.2 percent of violent incidents took place in maximum custody settings. In early 1973 (prior to the "lockdown" of California prisons), 11 percent of the violent incidents occurred in special housing. After major shifts into security housing, the proportion of incidents there increased to 47 percent, while violence in lower custody settings decreased correspondingly.

[c]A.L. Guenther [55], who studied inmate violence in two federal institutions, reports that conflicts involving homosexuality were the most frequent cause of assaults on inmates in the prison he surveyed. Guenther's study comprises a six-year period (1968–74 fiscal years). Ellis et al. conclude from their North Carolina survey that "sex is regarded as an important instigator to aggression in both youth and adult prisons" [45, p. 32].

[d]This summary, and those below, are prepared from narratives in routine Incident Reports submitted to the California Department of Corrections. They are relatively typical of incidents whose cause is known.

forcefully than norms call for. Extreme violence in rapes is also found in prison; aggressive rapists seem to regard terror as more essential to creating a climate of receptivity in men than in women.

Following a heated altercation between inmates S and L, S obtains a razor blade, enters L's cell, and cuts L about the face and chest. S testifies that L had visited him to involve him in homosexual activities, and had been pressuring him. Other inmate sources point out that S has been under pressure from several homosexuals.

Inmate A sits in C's cell listening to C play his guitar; four other inmates enter. The situation looks sufficiently unpromising for A to attempt an exit, but he is stopped as he tries to leave. He gets a beating from C (which fractures his jaw). Following this beating, A is forced to lie down on the floor, where C performs sodomy on him. After lunch, A is "escorted" back to A's cell, where another inmate (M) rapes him.

Displays of force and acts of panic permeate prison violence. Force is displayed to regulate covenants. It backs small property claims, contracts, gambling debts. The civil justice of the yard prescribes deterrence through capital punishment. The insolvent is fair game:

JR owes RR several cartons of cigarettes. (RR reports that this debt covers gambling losses; JR insists he has been paying for protection.) RR gives JR two months to settle, but JR is unable to do so; the best he can do is supply several hobby shop lamps, which only cover half of the amount owed. At the end of the two-month period, JR is stabbed in the yard by M, who is frequently used by RR to "collect debts."

H is stabbed to death in a shower room, with L doing the stabbing, and D holding H until he collapses. H had owed L five cartons of cigarettes, and also had incurred a debt (of 15 packs) with D. L indicates that he had decided that if H "did not pay me the cigarettes he owed me, I was going to kill him." He stabbed H some 16 times, and explains that "I wanted to kill the guy. The mother f----r deserved it."

Beyond the use of violence to back "valid" contracts, it is sometimes deployed to promote expropriation. The inmate subculture relates to such violence neutrally or passively; exploitation is regarded as a "private" matter. It calls for noninvolvement by those without ties or a stake in the transaction:

Inmate A has made a name for himself as "dumb hillbilly," and this is viewed as an invitation to extort cigarettes from him. One inmate approaches him and informs him that if he does not deliver two cartons of cigarettes "we'll get the s--t on." A replies that he owes no cigarettes, and has no objection if this should lead to a fight. The next day he is stabbed in the back while on his way to his cell.

L attacks C in a large community group meeting, first using fists, and then a knife. L claims that C had stolen a pair of street shoes from him the previous evening, and when requested to return same, had responded, "You know you aren't getting the shoes back, sucker."

Both "legitimate" and "private" uses of violence are protected by the taboo against informing, which extends to the victim. The taboo—like other norms—is reinforced by threat of violence. This threat includes the possibility of snitch suspects being attacked on the basis of poorly documented suspicion:

C has been identified to authorities as having exerted homosexual pressure on several inmates—among others, J. As a result of this information, C is assigned temporarily to the Adjustment Center. After C is released from this assignment, he hunts for inmates whom he suspects of having informed against him. He encounters J, and stabs him in the shoulder, since he mistakenly assumes that J was one of the informers.

Inmate B is released from his daily exercise period, requisitions a "long-handled, heavy duty brush," and assaults inmate attendant O with this utensil. He testifies that he "felt that O had been 'snitching' on him, that O was the cause of his cell having been searched by custodial personnel."

The use of violence against suspected informers is permitted, but not necessarily prescribed. If it were, prison yards would be soaked in blood. The same point holds of the most common form of violence—the avenging of insults. The abstract rule condemns men who permit themselves, or their friends, to be slighted. A nonavenger—like a noncollector of debts—may decrease his stature, and may risk a reputation of nonself-sufficiency. But the seriousness of the insult, and the wisdom of retaliation, are matters of individual discretion. Violent revenge is the private act of the aggrieved party. If revenge provokes counter-retaliation, the counter aggressor gains the same protection from his peers as his victim. A man is protected, although not respected, even if his retaliation is non-commensurate with his slight:

CA is in debt to CH, and CH requests at least partial repayment. CA replies by becoming abusive, and CH tells him to "forget about it," and follows CH to the bathroom, where he subjects him to "vile names." CH administers one blow to CA, which knocks the latter unconscious. CA is only 4'11" tall, is very conscious of his size, and is known as "Toughy" among friends. When several inmates make remarks to him about the bathroom incident, he is unable to cope with these, and decides to take "revenge." The next day, he approaches CH, who is seated at a table, and stabs him twice.

Three months before, a "racial disturbance" had occurred between Negro inmates and inmates of Mexican origin, in another institution. One member of the "Mexican" group (6), had been killed, and the suspicion fell on L, a member of the Negro clique. After this incident, several members of both factions were transferred to their current location. Then, in succession, (1) S, a close friend of

L, is stabbed while passing through a group of "Mexicans"; inmate C is known to be responsible for this stabbing; (2) C is stabbed to death by unknown assailants.

Beyond inmate norms, men are subjected to assigned roles and obligations of their clique or subgroup. These pressures may be especially intense. In group-centered conflicts, aggressors see themselves as appointed group agents. Violence is sparked by shared affronts. Men qualify as victims by belonging to an enemy group. Although a violent incident may be contrived (by a specially strongly motivated group member) counterretaliations and counter-counterretaliations may involve increasingly random participants:

During a period of racial tension, a clique of white prisoners had issued an ultimatum to blacks, prohibiting them from entering the T.V. room. Black inmate T resolved to "lead his people" (against everyone's advice) by watching television. T and C enter the T.V. room, and are immediately assaulted with some homemade blackjacks by a group of whites. Staff prevents the murder of the two men.

While walking along a corridor, Inmate M (a "Mexican") is knocked unconscious by a black inmate. The next evening, several inmates of Mexican origin push a black as the latter leaves the T.V. room. "This causes the races to group and arm themselves." Chairs are thrown, and men are hit with socks containing soap. The battle is averted by the staff.

Although aggressors in group-retaliation incidents sometimes act in self-appointed fashion, most are encouraged by their peers. They may also view violence as a duty inherent in their formal group role. Even in early California surveys, prison aggressors were sometimes described as "suspected gang leader."

The peer culture facilitates assaults. Rather than *specifically* encouraging attacks on a *particular* victim, it increases the respectability of attacking certain *categories* of victims such as informers and welchers.

Ultimately, it is up to the aggressor to classify himself as facing or not facing a provocation. The aptness of his decision subsequently translates into a consensus or lack of consensus of peers. An "execution" for nonpayment may be less admired if the aggressor is a notorious loanshark, than if he is acting on behalf of a friend who has been blatantly betrayed. A man who violates an ethical norm, such as by treacherously stabbing his victim in the back without notice, may be condemned, although the occasion for his violence, such as snitching, may be respectable.

Whether or not an inmate assault receives inmate approval, it can enjoy support—as with the police—in the form of nonintervention or silence. This subcultural reinforcement, on which the aggressor can count, plays a role in producing violence, because it *withholds controls that deter violence*. It protects the assaultive inmate—as it does the violent police officer—because survival concerns are more critical to a man's peers than norms that circumscribe or limit violence.

The evidence suggests that different institutions have different problems of violence. Retaliatory stabbings of randomly selected inmates by representatives of warring groups may occur in a self-consciously segregated population in which rival predators live in fear of reciprocal aggression. In other institutions violence may involve contractual executions by members of rival syndicates. Where special situations or groupings are absent, the traditional range of violent incidents can be expected.

This fact holds in California today. Thus, Ziegler [199] observes that Folsom Prison—a California institution for long termers—has produced few group conflicts:

Folsom can in no way be characterized as seething with revolutionary fever. As a matter of fact, overall political consciousness rates about .08 on a scale of 10, and a black guerrilla would receive about as much support as a real live gorilla running loose in the yard.... In Folsom, blacks, browns and whites live together in easy harmony without fear or racial strife. This peace has endured for a year, in spite of two incidents (the stabbing of a black by whites, and the stabbing of a Chicano by a black) which in more turbulent times would have exploded into bloody conflict.... The same old rules still apply in (Folsom) prison: don't gamble, or snitch, or mess around with narcotics or sissies, don't go to the hospital and you will live to a ripe old age [199, pp. 67-68].

In December of 1973, several California prisons had produced such high rates of violence that they were "locked down"—with inmates restricted to their cells or confined to segregation. The impact of this experiment suggests that specialized conflicts may respond more easily to suppression than the ordinary range of prison incidents. Pre and postlockdown comparisons show "gang reprisals" reduced, with no reduction in violence classified as "commodity" (debts and gambling), "individual" (disputes or arguments), and "unknown." In another typology "racial" and "clique" stabbings show decreases as a result of the lockdown, but "individual" stabbings register increases.

The criminal justice system has impact on prison assaults. In California, for example, the parole board (Adult Authority) "has become tougher in granting paroles and quicker to revoke them for violations" [115]. Such a policy creates bitterness, and removes the deterrent force of disciplinary actions. An inmate who is deprived of his release date if he acts out may well be cautious about how he conducts himself. He may well become indifferent to his fate, however, if parole decisions are so conservative that no further loss of freedom is produced by violence.

"Decarceration" policies thus can have a double impact on assaults in prisons. While they operate to fill prisons with men who are aggressive, tough, or bitter, they can also reduce (through restrictive parole) the stakes that these men have in remaining nonviolent.

Assaults on Staff

Decarceration creates a situation in which well-matched, tough inmates face each other in the yard, and in which staff must labor to "control" men who see themselves entitled to more autonomy than traditional inmates.

In the traditional inmate culture, antistaff aggressors were held in contempt by their peers as threats to group security [170]. Today's prison populations—particularly those of younger offenders—have generated norms that can make vocal attacks on staff or refusals to obey staff orders status conferring. These norms may call for assertions of autonomy in the face of custodial "disrespect," and may prescribe resistance to acts defined as discriminatory or unfair.

Attacks on staff in past years tended to feature inmates whose angry, excited, or frustrated state of mind (usually temporary) made them oblivious to risk, or inmates who were already exposed to serious risk through staff action. Two incidents, cited by Guenther [55], are typical of such occasions:

Abransom 67977 and Radtke 91113 were observed to be highly inebriated in their cellhouse quarters. When asked to accompany the officer to the Lieutenant's office they became hostile and had to be physically removed to Segregation.

Maitland 58296 threatened an officer, Mr. Fravega, after his supply of "christmas trees" (drugs) was confiscated. Maitland was subdued and taken to Segregation. (p. 27)

A third incident described by Guenther is of a new and different order. While it involves paranoid fear, it suggests a tendency for the aggressor to define staff actions as illegitimate, and as calling for a violent response:

Harding 47619 in Cellhouse B accused the officer of spitting in his oatmeal, and of racial prejudice. He threw his tray against the wall and refused to move from the cell. When officers arrived to move him he attacked Mr. Elliott, Mr. Tangerman, and Mr. Inglis. (p. 21)

Some observers characterize incidents of this kind as "politically" motivated. The validity of such a characterization hinges on the definition of "political." To the extent to which an inmate questions an officer's judgment, he raises issues of authority; but unless he challenges the decisions of *all* officers, which is seldom the case, his focus is on the legitimacy of specific acts. The inmate's premise that he has the right to differentiate among formally legitimized custodians is a challenge to the prison system, but it is personal, in that it involves criteria of individual officer conduct toward the inmate himself. It is no different from a suspect's reaction to a police contact, which—while it may be viewed by the officer as an affront to enforcement—is really an interpersonal conflict. Unlike police, however, custodial staff has much less experience with challenges to their personal decisions, and is thus more prone to draw the inference that the target of the challenges is prison law and order.

The picture of the "political" inmate is strengthened by a tendency of inmates to couch grievances along racial or legalistic lines. Such rhetoric is especially inviting because it is more respectable than confessing fear, or than facing the fact that one is not getting along with a guard. Moreover, legalistic reasoning (based on the issue of equity or systematic discrimination) leaves men in authority feeling visibly vulnerable. According to Mathieson [82], Norwegian prisoners have found it effective to invoke their keepers' rules in their complaints; Redl and Wineman [143] have shown that legalistically couched grievances are a skillful ego defense against rehabilitative staff.

Confrontation tactics can snowball. Where defenses provoke defenses, polarizations and escalations occur. Loss of control by one or another party can produce overt violence, which recycles as well. This is illustrated by a recent California trial involving inmates who had been labelled "violence prone" and sequestered in segregation. The attorney general in this trial "produced a spate of reports from prison officials in which Mr. D. was accused of flouting regulations, insulting and attacking guards and inciting fellow inmates to violence." The defendant alleged that "charges were false, and that he had only acted in 'self-defense' on these occasions, adding 'if I feel the rules are unjust I'm not going to abide by them'" [121]. Given these interlocking perspectives, a "flouting–inciting" versus "self-defense" cycle is played out, with escalations reflecting cumulating grievances.

Two factors have contributed to the bitterness of zero-sum games in which staff see themselves provoked by clients who perceive themselves harassed. One such factor is the weakening of the belief in the legitimacy of staff authority. This presumption is not confined to prisons; a psychiatrist attached to Bellevue Hospital, for instance, writes that:

As head of an adolescent ward which draws chiefly from the urban ghettos, I have observed a distinct change in the attitudes and feelings with which a doctor is regarded. Formerly held almost in awe, he came to be, in the years under consideration, a frequent object of contempt, as were all other symbols of authority. The attending psychiatrist with the longest experience of those attacked put it this way: My advice is stop wearing white coats! It used to open every door in the most remote slum areas of the city and an intern could feel safe wherever he went. Today it's the reverse and seems to evoke hostility everywhere [67, p. 7].

The second factor is the difficulty that some inmates have of interpreting interpersonal encounters with staff in other than ethnic terms. It is difficult to deescalate conflicts in which both parties see themselves goaded and attacked by racists. The task becomes impossible when each side sees confirmation of its views in the premise of the other.

The conflicting perceptions of staff and inmates may be reinforced by interested bystanders. A California prison psychiatrist, for example, characterized inmates who had thrown feces at guards as striving for self-actualization. "It's the only thing left to do," the psychiatrist declared. "It's humiliating to (the inmate), but it's the ultimate humiliation to a guard. He's just trying to say, 'I'm alive, I'm a human being, even if I don't act like one'" [101].

The problem is compounded by the fact that the prisons have inherited militant religious organizations, "self-help" groups, and in-house chapters of community groups. Such enclaves have been protected through court action, over staff objections. They are often the objects of reluctant toleration and watchful suspicion by staff. Members of such groups can irritate staff from their protected sanctuaries through militant rhetoric, and staff can try to restrict their operations. But violence is not a necessary outcome of such conflict; it is, rather, a by-product of aberrant escalations, or, more frequently, of self-appointed, uncontrolled members' acts.

The relationship between subcultural values and private motives is illustrated by an incident in Holmesburg Prison, in which a warden and deputy warden were stabbed to death by two Muslim inmates who had requested a hearing to complain "that they were not being given sufficient time to hold prayer services" [110]. The aggressors may have been Muslims, but—more significantly—they were men who had past histories of irrational violence against authority figures, both having been convicted of killing police officers. Their explosion in the warden's office was an expression of personal irrationality, but in response to their idiosyncratic actions, 235 black militant inmates were classified as violence prone and transferred. Moreover, the Pennsylvania legislature passed a bill restoring the death penalty for murder of prison staff.

Staff Violence

Inmates sometimes regale their attorneys or specially sympathetic outsiders with stories of organized guard brutality. Stereotyped accounts come in several shapes, including a "thumps-and-screams-in-the-cell-next-door" variety, a "blood-dripping-stretcher" version, and the "Supreme Beatup" claim. Such stories are mostly untrue, but are hard to disconfirm, because prisons release no data about staff uses of legitimate force.

Correctional systems (like police) have access to relatively good information about incidents involving serious injury. This is the case because if an incident is not reported, this increases vulnerability in the event of claims or suits. In most jurisdictions the picture of guard violence is not alarming. In New York State, for instance, 386 incidents (involving 547 inmates and 1,288 employees) are documented for 1973 [97]. The number is modest, because it provides 15,000 inmates a probability of one staff confrontation a day. Moreover, while in a third of the incidents no one suffered injuries, in the remaining conflicts the damage consisted of scratches, bruises, bumps, swellings, or discolorations. The most frequent type of force that was employed was the "hold," defined as "nelson, choke, grab, pull . . . all wrestling holds." And the most frequently cited reason for staff violence was the effort to "prevent serious injury to other persons or property."

In New York State prisons, in the typical incident of staff violence against inmates, a fight is broken up—more often than not by a group of officers. But this picture excludes data about significant variations on the theme. "Prevention of force" is the justificatory formula for guard violence. It is a formula similar to those employed by police to document "reasonableness" of restraint. Reform is precluded if a more accurate analysis of problem situations and responses is unavailable. More important, the few violence-generating guards we know exist (and whose presence may be no secret to staff) cannot be pinpointed unless incidents are tabulated so that we can locate repeaters. Other data, such as testimony by peers, are unavailable, because a combination of unionization and subcultural pressures covers the violence-prone guard with a blanket of silence as effectively as it does the aggressive patrolman or the violent inmate.

It is also clear that the standard portrait of the guard is not universally applicable. Subcultures of violence can exist among guards ("goon squads") to whom conflict-related work is delegated. More informally, staff can become apprehensive, "hard-nosed," or caught in vendettas. If these violence pockets are not addressed with full regard to their special dynamics, they may stigmatize and demoralize the uninvolved.

Physical confrontations between guards and inmates can generate fear among both inmates and staff. Jacobs and Retsky [63] note in an essay on prison guards that fear is a latent theme in the guard culture even under ordinary circumstances:

The guard's world has increasingly come to be pervaded by fear and uncertainty. . . . Tension continually looms over the prison threatening to explode into assault or even riot. This is drilled into the recruit during his first training classes. The guard's manual stresses the need for vigilance and alertness lest the unexpected take one unaware. Not only is the new guard exposed to the word-of-mouth stories of fellow students and training officers, but at the prison he immediately may be exposed to situations which confirm his worst fears. (p. 22)

Jacobs and Retsky [63] also note that like police, "few prison guards speak openly about fear, though they attribute such concerns to their wives and families" (p. 23). Also, like police, guards judge inmates "on how willingly they conform to authority. . . . The 'no good' inmate causes trouble for the guard by insisting on his rights and privileges; mail, medicine, telephone calls, and the like" (p. 26).[e]

---

[e]The guards' concern with "authority" issues is also documented in a recent study by Shrom [158].

The "authority" issue arises particularly because of the custodial definitions of the officers' job. The ACA *Corrections Officers Training Guide* [3], for example, lists the following duties as comprising the work of guard personnel:

1. Supervises inmates in the housing units
2. Supervises inmates assembled for chapel, for entertainment, and for athletic contests
3. Supervises groups of inmates during serving of meals
4. Supervises groups of inmates assembled for baths and exchange of clothing
5. Supervises inmates during recreational periods
6. Supervises work performance of inmates
7. Supervises visits to prisoners
8. Exercises disciplinary control over inmates
9. Inspects inmates person and quarters for contraband
10. Maintains outer perimeter security
11. Prevents or controls fights between inmates
12. Controls and restrains inmates
13. Handles emergencies
14. Hears inmate grievances and counsels inmates
15. Operates and inspects security devices
16. Cares for equipment
17. Escorts visitors through the institution
18. Transports inmates (pp. 16-18)

Only one item on the list (#14) envisages a relationship other than adversary or supervisory between officers and inmates. No provision is made for positive personal contact, or for the exercise of interpersonal skills—other than leadership —by the officer. The development of relationships between inmates and officers may, in fact, be specifically prohibited. The *N.Y. State Department of Correctional Services Employee Handbook* [98], for example, specifically states (in section 5·4) that:

5.4: no employee shall engage in any conversation, communication, dealing, transaction, association, or relationships with any inmate or former inmate or any visitor, friends or relative of any inmate or former inmate in any manner or form which is not necessary or proper for the discharge of the employee's duties. (p. 34)

Such archaic rules may not be literally applied by correctional administrators. But they translate into subcultural norms, which are counterparts to the "never talk to a screw" rule of inmates. To the extent to which such norms are operative, they help to create a trench warfare climate in the prison yard.

Inmate Self-inflicted Violence

Prison violence is not necessarily directed at other men. The most frequent victims of violence in prison are self-mutilators, whose plight—except for completed suicides—draws no sympathy. Such victims are viewed as unmanly by peers, and as weaklings by staff. Self-injuries are also equated with petty manipulation and aid seeking.

Frieda Fromm Reichmann tells us, with regard to self-injuries generally, that:

Any patient who has made a suicidal attempt must be approached . . . as a person who has felt unhappy, incapacitated, discouraged or desperate enough to actually try to end his own life. A thorough investigation of the validity of the causes for the patient's discouragement, unhappiness or despair must be the starting point. . . . There is a fallacy . . . that an unsuccessful suicidal attempt is indicative of the fact that the patient was not serious in his suicidal intention. . . . The number of patients who stage a suicidal attempt to attract attention is negligibly small. But anyone so lacking in self-respect, so unhappy, so lonely, or mentally disordered, that he despairs of getting attention by means other than attempted suicide must be equally in need of . . . help [50, p. 198].

Contrary to stereotypes, most inmate self-injuries reflect concrete and intense personal breakdowns [175]. Most frequently, these are crises of self-doubt, hopelessness, fear, or abandonment. There are also psychotic crises—problems of self-management, tension, delusions, or panic. At best, self-directed violence mirrors helplessness, and involves coping problems with no perceived solution. Crises vary with type of population. They are more prevalent among youths than among older inmates, and among white and Latin inmates. Prisons feature different crises than jails; married inmates, for instance, feel more vulnerable in jail, while single inmates suffer more heavily in prison. Ethnic, sex, and age groups differ in their special vulnerabilities. Latin inmates, for example, are often acutely upset if they feel abandoned by relatives; women have problems with loneliness, or with the management of their feelings.

Prisons as living environments cannot control the stresses they may tend to produce. Different inmates react to different aspects of their imprisonment as particularly stressful. While some men are susceptible to the press of isolation, others react to crowding, conflict, inactivity, coldness, or the aggressive challenges of peers.

Whatever the shape of a man's crisis, the institution has no truck with it when the inmate reacts with self-inflicted violence. The yard's measure of esteem is manliness.[f] Self-injury means despair, and despair is unmanly. The inmate-in-crisis must deny his problems to survive. Others must deny them too.

---

[f]Women's institutions are more sympathetic to the expression of feelings, but tend to foster regression and dependence.

If problems are recognized, the inmate is stigmatized. If they are not recognized, he is abandoned.

Violent Games

Although the concern of this book is with physical acts, our portrait must touch —this once—on verbal conduct. For prisons and jails are permeated by violent talk, which leaves inmates depressed, unsure, and panic stricken.

We have noted that new inmates are often subject to threats that center on the prospect of being robbed or raped. Such overtures have impact. Inmates learn to doubt their adequacy as human beings. Huffman [60] refers to young men who were hospitalized as a result of "situational reactions to homosexual advances."

Homosexual threats are not uniformly distributed in prison. In his survey of rapes, Davis [39] provides a profile that seems to hold for verbal threats. This profile suggests that

1. Victims tend to be white.
2. Victims tend to be younger and smaller than aggressors.
3. Most victims are afraid to report their aggressors to the authorities.
4. Virtually every person having the characteristics of a potential victim is approached sexually by aggressors.
5. Aggressors tend to be black.
6. Aggressors tend to be guilty of more serious and more assaultive felonies than victims.
7. Both aggressors and victims tend to be younger than other prison inmates. (pp. 14-15)

Victims are selected for perceived physical and psychological characteristics. These features relate to norms endorsed by veterans of street gangs and juvenile institutions [62, p. 28]. Such men see themselves as extremely male, and as entitled to sexual gratification in an ascendent–submissive relationship with a "nonmale." This frame of reference has been traced to the emasculating impact of prison [51, 76, 188], but more plausibly relates to subcultural norms that inmates import into prison [60, 62].

Victims must conform to the aggressor's image of nonmanliness or femaleness. In the words of Buffum (who paraphrases Ward),

The "punks" are those who don't fight, who are dependent, who are "queer". It is the physical weaklings against whom the masculinity of those who are stronger is pointed [25, p. 16].

Ethnicity is incidental to this formula, and reflects an assumption often made by sophisticated black inmates that young white first offenders are particularly likely to be weak, fearful, unpugnacious, *and therefore unmanly.* Targets may be selected because they look "female" (slight, young, shy); but they are pursued because their reactions to threats and overtures reinforce a diagnosis of unmanliness. Such a diagnosis is made where the victim looks resourceless, seems unable or unwilling to engage in aggressive repartee, and has no "manly" partners or friends.

There is a two-fold tragedy here. First, inmates who are most susceptible to victimization are the most inviting targets for it; and the more obviously a man suffers, the less he is able to defend himself, the more likely he is to be pursued. Second, the norms of the game—those of manliness—protect the aggressor. Since the aggressors conform to the dominant manly concerns of prisons, their victims are unlikely to find solace or aid among peers, or among staff.

Collective Violence

Riots may be labelled "prison violence," but experts who study riots rarely center on the violence of riots. Explanations of riots, which tend to center on grievances, communication blocs, system change, explain collective behavior, but do not necessarily help us understand the violence—if any—that riots entail.

Aside from vandalism, riots feature (1) catalytic incidents, which tend to be staff–inmate confrontations, (2) private violent acts committed under color of rioting (rapes or executions of suspected informants), (3) violence used by authorities to quell riots, and (4) retaliatory behavior by prison staff following the riot.

Catalytic incidents profit from climate factors. Escalating misunderstandings between inmates and staff lend credibility to grossly distorting rumors, which can translate a fight or an arrest into an impending massacre. Such incidents may also include participants who are unrepresentatively demonstrative or aggressive inmates or staff.

Rapes or retaliatory acts committed during riots are probably equivalent to similar acts under nonriot conditions. Although opportunities for incidents may increase through the lifting of staff control, this does not mean that new types of violence need emerge.

It is also plausible that staff violence disproportionately features staff members who are otherwise violence prone. If a charge is ordered against hostage-holding rioters, violence is not a necessary product of the decision. There are those who break ranks, or shoot first, or attack less discriminately than others. And administrators who order confrontations may respond to norms of machismo ("never give in"), warfare ("we don't negotiate with inmates"), or fear ("there'd be a bloodbath").

Subcultural motives are most salient in the postriot conduct of guards. In such outbursts, as in "police riots," staff respond to situational pressures, such as fear, rumor, reactions to affront, and group loyalties. It is true that such violence would not occur in ordinary situations. But the forces unleashed are, in the final analysis, the normative themes we discuss throughout this book.

The Impact of Violence

Prison violence, like other violence, affects more than its victims. The typical aggressors—mostly, hard-care offenders—reinforce the worst in themselves. Their success strengthens their premise that violence is the means to life's goals, that toughness buys status, and that terror "sells." Aggression makes the abuse of others the measure of pride; it cements membership in retaliatory or predatory groups. It confirms staff stereotypes of clients, which translate into fear, suppression, disdain.

Staff suffers in other respects. Although there is little impact to staff repressive measures, the illusion of control persists. It demands public pretense and private cynicism. It brings increasingly indiscriminate enforcement and scapegoating. Inmates who are punished—those caught clinging to the iceberg's tip— are (understandably) embittered. They may react with hate. Others continue to "do their own time." To do so means to close one's eyes, one's heart, and one's mind. It means self-centered values, parochial loyalties, noncommunity. It insures psychological survival, but at the expense of dehumanization.

The public is similarly affected. Our concern with violence awakens only when violence threatens to spill over prison walls. Even then, we tend to delude ourselves. We see prison violence as spontaneous and perverse. We make no allowance for the fact that the orientation of our prisons may itself help to produce violence—violence that responds to a control and warfare model that we perpetuate, stipulate, and support.

5 Conflict Management in Prisons

As is the case with the police, violence reduction efforts in prison can take a great many forms, which depend on assumptions that are made about violence, about management, and about change. Prisons can claim to engage in violence control when they introduce guard towers, segregate inmates, provide refresher courses to guards, experiment with grievance procedures, or expand psychiatric services.

Four different problems are addressed in prison where "violence" is at issue. These problems are (1) inmate riots, (2) force used by custodial staff, (3) convict assaults on other convicts, and (4) violence committed by ex-inmates.

Of these concerns, the most consistent worry of prison administrators relates to potential riots. Riots and their prevention have traditionally been translated into security concerns. It has been customary that if a prison mess hall is obliterated by rioters, the new mess hall comes equipped with a steel-enclosed outpost for armed guards, or additional locks and gates. "Lessons" derived from each riot have centered around deficient security, riot equipment, or combat options. "Prevention" has translated into filling perceived security voids so as physically to deter future rioters, and to enable staff to respond to riots with more force, speed, and presumed efficacy.

While some present-day administrators still perceive riots as military problems, others have new and broader perspectives. Where their concern is still the prevention of violence, their answer is not merely to take greater security measures and deploy greater force. "Keeping the lid on" means more to these administrators than locking prisons down and doubling guard shifts. It includes reforms designed to improve prison conditions and calculated to neutralize inmate grievances.

Some social scientists assume that prison staff have not known—until these same social scientists told them—that riots relate to accumulated resentment, unmet needs, or perceived inequities. One forgets that inmate riot demands have always featured rosters of poor food, supervision, classification or medical care [162].

The change we see in prison is not born of new knowledge, but of new assumptions about staff-client relationships. "Old" wardens saw inmates as recipients of obligations and benefits. If food or nursing were temporarily substandard, inmates were seen as having to accept these facts until staff decided—on its own—to effect improvements. Where inmates complained, staff

65

could listen, comply or refuse, or discipline the complainer. If they reacted adversely, it was because the inmate implied, through the tenor of his approach, that he challenged the right of his keepers to determine conditions of his captivity. Where petitions might be accepted, demands were not.

Riots were analogously viewed. While staff might admit the legitimacy of riot-related complaints, they viewed riots as inadmissible challenges to their authority. The logic dictated that even where reforms were already contemplated, they must be suspended if rioters demanded them. Implementation of riot demands could occur later, *provided* they were dissociated from riots.

This view still holds. "No concessions to force" is a popular correctional stance [2]. While agreements may be signed to save lives, there is no compunction—as in the Jackson Prison Riot—about breaking one's word. Reforms then occur, at staff whim, when memory of the demands, and of the concessions, wanes.

The inflexibility of this staff stance has two sources: There is the issue of authority, which equates compromise with surrender or weak control. And there is the "deterrence" view: Riots occur, this view holds, when riots "work." Where inmates see riot demands being met, their next route to improvement will be rioting. Discontent must translate to violence.

Although this view is superficially persuasive, it is empirically unproved and psychologically suspect. The portrait of goal-oriented, pragmatic, and rational rioters ignores the last-resort quality of collective violence. It ignores the cumulation of preriot grievances. It ignores built-in controls—custodial and peer pressures—which discourage riots. And where the view overrates inmate pragmatism, it underrates staff investments. The deterrence argument is testable. Staff machismo (the need for control) is not. For it is a fact that staff does not control inmates, and that we know this. Gresham Sykes [170] noted that "the dominant position of the custodial staff is more fiction than reality, if we think of domination as something more than the outward forms of power" (p. 45). Most inmates accept much of prison as a given. But inmates need not continue to accept prison conditions in the future. Inmates have the potential of resisting staff authority, and if this happens, staff become powerless.

Riots reveal staff powerlessness, because they commit staff to their last gambit, which is violence. Even enlightened administrators are hard put to attend to riot-framed grievances. Riots create a situation where grievances are inappropriately framed ("nonnegotiable") or overladen with riot-created overtones, such as amnesty demands, which override the preriot issues requiring solution. Simulated negotiations, such as a recent NCCD-sponsored experiment [134], suggest the possibility of arbitrating riots, but real-life riots introduce emotional investments and consequences of rioting that make constructive resolutions very difficult.

Defusing Grievances

It is not surprising that the enlightened administrator feels that he must find solutions to inmate grievance before escalation occurs. The movement to institute grievance procedures in prisons arises in this context, as a self-conscious violence-prevention effort. It is based on the premise that "unresolved grievances have caused collective violence, riot, and disorder in correctional institutions" [163]. It presumes that if the preconditions of violence are addressed, volatile incidents become powerless as stimuli that spark collective disturbances.

There is more to the current approach, however, than the defusing of discontent. New procedures confer on inmates the right to draw third parties into transactions with staff. The third-party role (grievance adjudication) is new in its nonadversary problem-solving focus. It redefines challenges of power into questions of substance, where the merit of the claim is the point at issue. It forces inmates to argue the equity of their cause, and forces staff to state the rationale of their decisions. In this new context, machismo loses some of its dominant hold over the way staff–inmate games are played.

What grievance procedures tend to do is to help staff relate to inmates (and vice-versa) in nonconfrontation terms. The inmate with a grievance is an agent of conflict. If Jones wants to grow a mustache he plays a prescribed, standard role. His argument goes, "Staff has no right to dictate my shaving habits; I'm emasculated by malevolent tyrants. Men resist tyranny. Do your worst!" Staff–who have no prior investment in clean-shaven lips–feel attacked and challenged. Their reaction ("mustaches are a security problem; one can hide a knife in a large mustache") ring hollow. The ostensible issue becomes the proving ground of manhood. Irrespective of outcome, a residue of bitterness and suspicion is inevitable. A third.party can prevent this outcome, by offering solutions that may be face saving ("mustaches may be worn if less than ten inches in length") and are not cast in zero-sum (staff loses, inmate wins) terms. Most important, the grievance process provides models that can transfer–without the need for intermediaries–to staff–inmate relations generally.

The Prison Ombudsman

Inmates and their keepers are traditionally at stalemate, but they have no monopoly on this realm. The role of government anywhere translates uneasily into warm acceptance by the governed.

One effort to close the credibility gap between government and the governed was instituted 200 years ago in Sweden. It consists of a citizen representative–the ombudsman–who is concerned with correcting governmental mistakes and abuses. The ombudsman's role circumvents standard channels, when these are exhausted. It permits any citizen to file a complaint against any official, with the assurance of investigation and review.

The Scandinavian ombudsman is a man with power. He is a source of critique, and an engineer of reform. His jurisdiction is unlimited, and his independence complete.

In Scandinavia, ombudsmen respond to petitions from inmates as well as other citizens. About 400 complaints from prisons were reviewed by Sweden's ombudsman in 1973, and "prisoners are among (the Danish) ombudsman's most frequent clients" [141, p. 57]. In the United States, where prisons are used more than elsewhere in the world, there is room for special prison ombudsmen, who can process inmate grievances in major prisons or prison systems.

The role of the prison ombudsman is usually generously defined. The job announcement for the ombudsman position in Holmesburg Prison of Pennsylvania, for example, reads:

The Ombudsman will work within prison walls, handling individual grievances, determining the extent of individual and organizational problems, and attempting to solve such problems by recommendation, direct action, or appropriate referral. This position will fall outside the normal prison chain of command [34, p. 174].

Although riots can be a motive for proposing ombudsmen (as was the case in Holmesburg) the objectives of the experiment can be more broadly envisaged. The Philadelphia Corrections Development Project states the aims of its Ombudsman proposal as

1. Serving to protect the prisoner from official error and abuse
2. Advising prison administration of developing problems within the institution.
3. Functioning as a preventive influence by encouraging inmates to "ventilate" in a constructive manner
4. Assist the prison administration in resolving correction-related problems requiring legislative change or action beyond the administrative scope of the prison system [34, p. 169].

Two of these items (1 and 3) focus on inmate–staff relationships, and two others (2 and 4) imply organizational change. The ombudsman ideally is not only a man who can peacefully resolve destructive conflicts, but a person who can deal with organizational forces that promote conflicts.

Ombudsmen in prisons face two problems: One is to gain the trust of inmates; the other is to neutralize the fear or the resentment of staff. Both subcultural views can defeat ombudsmen from the start. Staff can define the new role as subversive, as a danger to their job security. Whenever an inmate's requests are denied, the ombudsman can buttress the inmate's cynicism, suspicion, and felt impotence. The ombudsman can be seen as the staff "fink" who creates a smokescreen for nonexistent options, and he can become, for staff, a free-wheeling executioner who is hired to fire staff who incur the disfavor of inmates.

A skilled, well-backed ombudsman can neutralize his stigmata over time. To do so, he must be open to legitimate grievances, but not to petty, spurious, or scurrilous ones. He must make it known to all parties that he is not subject to manipulation, and that he is unwilling to become enmeshed with vendettas, dependency bids, and professional complaining. The ombudsman must prove that his detached stance permits insight into staff–inmate conflicts and that this insight can benefit inmates, staff, and administrators alike. Superintendents do need "objective" facts and disinterested counsel. Inmates do need catharsis, and the chance to discuss core adjustment problems. And staff can use help with interpersonal difficulties and with procedures that may boomerang. The ombudsman who "sells" integrity responds to organizational needs. He is more than a supplement to grievance machinery and communication networks. He is an agent of change.

Ten of the 14 prison ombudsmen currently active in the United States are correctional staff members. This affiliation creates an invitation to inmate skepticism. A Trenton, New Jersey inmate describes his ombudsman as "just a waste of time, because you know this guy is working for the administration. You can't expect the man to bite the hand that is signing his check" [83, p. 46].

Strangely enough (at first glance) an ombudsman's employment by a prison system reassures staff as little as it does inmates. In the New York Division for Youth, the ombudsman records that

a major factor in the loneliness of the Ombudsman is the hostility of staff. Prior to taking their positions, the Ombudsmen were made aware of the possibility of staff hostility, and they accepted this. However . . . the hostility was much deeper than . . . anticipated and . . . resulted in nearly complete isolation from other staff at the institutions they visited [83, p. 60].

All this means is that the ombudsman who is a staff member meets additional resistance to his work. He may have to spend more effort reassuring inmates of confidentiality, and staff of impartiality. But the crucial factor here is not the ombudsman's place in the table of organization; it is the safeguards he can offer to his clients. Ombudsmen, whether or not employed by a prison system, must buy or earn their credibility. They can do so by not leaking files, showing gullibility, welching on commitments, neglecting rapport, or shunning top-level backing.

As a change agent, the ombudsman faces unique problems. He is uninvited by his constituents. He enters the sort of games in which efforts to satisfy one party imply a threat to the other; where men are at war, and real fear is present;

where clients who approach the ombudsman (except to coopt him) may be viewed as weak, unself-sufficient, unmanly.

The facade of prison, however, sits uneasily, with strain and cost. Men may claim hate, but still want acceptance. They may want stability, safety, structure. Guises of manhood hide vulnerabilities. Egos sense their own deficits and needs. At some level, the Man Who Can Afford Not to Play the Game can provide escape for those who are captured by it.

The ombudsman who fails may not fail because he "worked for the administration," but because he saw himself as a staff or an inmate advocate. Conflict works for some change agents, such as for organizers who fight client passivity in the community, but partisanship can prove fatal where conflict norms distort perceptions and foreclose constructive solutions.

The converse (a nonconflict stance) emerges in success stories of ombudsman programs that work. In Minnesota, a corrections commissioner characterized an ombudsman in his state as a "nonbiased man with no hidden agenda. . . . W. happens to be a man without any (biases)." A prison union official testified concerning the same ombudsman that

the suspicion is gone. There's not that fear of "what's this guy after . . . what the hell is going on?" They're going to give everybody a fair shake. They're not just listening to the inmate . . . they're listening to everybody."

A warden praised the ombudsman as a "straight professional . . . an honest man . . . at least he understands our problems and how we think. He may not buy it, but he understands" [83, p. 48].

The Minnesota program bears evidence of the potential value of the ombudsman's role as a change agent. Among reforms instituted through an ombudsman's recommendation in this state were a staff-inmate advisory council and a procedure for disclosure, to inmates, of parole decisions. These and other results of the program have helped to reduce conflict and to relieve tension.

Connecticut used classic organizational change strategies from the inception of its program. It planned the ombudsman's role with participation from all of the ombudsman's constituencies, including correctional union members and inmates. This procedure helped various resistances to surface early. It also provided an opportunity for top staff to publicly endorse and back the ombudsman program.

From our perspective, ombudsmen can ameliorate violence-enhancing pressures on inmates and staff. The ombudsman is potentially free of the normative assumptions of prisons. He can thus solve problems that staff and inmates—who are caught in their respective subcultures—cannot address themselves.

Built-in Grievance Machinery

Prisons are often compared to boilers, in which violence occurs where tension accumulates. The lesson derived from this analog is that prisons must provide "safety valves" of a constructive or nonviolent sort [99]. The same point is derived from studies of collective violence generally. In the free world, dissatisfied men may explode after they have tried conventional remedies but have found these channels to be unresponsive [184].

In prisons, if inmates have grievances, they can present these to outside agencies, such as courts. Inmate appeals sometimes succeed at this level, but they may at the same time escalate conflicts in prisons. Famous inmate sagas (such as that of Martin Sostre) suggest that staff may retaliate against chronic writ writers with violence. And courts suffer from their status as "outsiders." They can legislate reform, but cannot insure implementation, because of

the less-than-enthusiastic responses of the top levels of administration to these forced changes. Without the forceful leadership and the full support of administrators in implementing court-decreed changes, only indecisiveness and confusion can result [61, p. 42].

It has been suggested elsewhere that "introducing adversariness and legal game-playing into the prison regime may do more to stimulate violence in prisons than to suppress it" [61, p. 43]. This contention cannot carry much weight if courts are the only road to much needed reform. But it suggests that prisons would do well to explore internal means of responding effectively to inmate complaints, and of initiating change.

The move for improved grievance procedure in prisons has been promoted by judges and by prestigious pressure groups. It is also favored by prison administrators. Denenberg and Denenberg [41] noted that as of 1972, most prisons had instituted new or modified grievance procedures.

The simplest sort of improvement deviates from former practices only in degree. It does so in (1) publicizing the availability of grievance mechanisms, (2) insuring that every complaint is attended to, (3) guaranteeing confidentiality, (4) providing for interviews and investigation, and (5) assuring full response to the complainant. Some of the programs also permit the inmate to secure peer assistance in formulating their grievance. Others provide for arbitration of special grievances.

The most distinct experiments, however, deviate qualitatively from systems that are now in use. These are the programs that are called "participatory." They are distinctive in that they provide for inmate involvement in the design of the experiment and/or in its implementation.

A good illustration is the effort of the California Youth Authority, whose director emphasizes that "kids who turn delinquent have a very keen sense of fairness." This premise suggests to the CYA that a climate of fairness must be invoked in treatment of youths [41, p. 41].

The Youth Authority program was designed at the Holton School for Delinquents by an inmate-staff committee, with consultant help. In this program, inmates can file complaints with an inmate "grievance clerk" elected by peers. Within five days, the issue is presented to a panel of staff and inmates:

The panel includes two elected wards, two staff members, and a non-voting chairman who may, if necessary, act as mediator. The grievance clerk also attends meetings. The grievant may represent himself or have another ward or staff member represent him at hearings [41, p. 44].

If an inmate is dissatisfied with the decision in his case, or if he objects to actions taken as a result of his complaint, he has the right to appeal. He selects one of the members of the Review Board, and the prison superintendent selects another. A third member is a labor arbitrator who makes his services available.

Unlike other procedures, which have not overcome skepticism, the Holton program is supported by inmates and staff. It seems to have raised morale, satisfied complainants, and (like the ombudsman) has pinpointed procedures in need of change.

Does grievance machinery reduce violence? In reviewing grievance procedures generally, Denenberg and Denenberg [41] conclude that:

Proponents of grievance procedures are reluctant to promote them as guarantees against riot. As one advocate remarked, "We could tell an administrator that if he sets up a grievance procedure the inmates won't burn the place down. But the first time the place burns down, we're out of business." A more realistic expectation, proponents say, is that grievance procedures will serve as one kind of safety valve, helping to eliminate friction while holding out the possibility of flowering into a system for governing prisons with at least partial consent of the governed. (p. 62)

The impact of new grievance procedures, including that of ombudsmen, is to undermine distortions and stereotypes that lead to violence [42]. In the arbitration process generally, the arbiter clears up misperceptions, identifies differences, provides "favorable . . . conditions for confronting the issues," encourages discussion, promotes "norms of rational interaction . . . and the desirability of reaching mutually satisfying agreement," suggests possible outcomes, sells "workable agreements," and makes the acceptance of new solutions "prestigeful and attractive to . . . the groups represented" [42, pp. 353-87].

This process prevents the escalation of issues it addresses. It insures that pork chops do not inspire riots, or that an inmate who feels himself harassed will consider coexisting with his guards. There can also be impact—through organizational change—on generic grievances or generalized concerns.

But none of this touches on core premises of inmate and staff cultures. Emerging issues are as likely as preceding ones to feature fear, suspicion, or power concerns. Grievance machineries never put themselves out of business; if anything, their success recruits new grievances.

Client participation opens different vistas. Participants learn and practice problem solving. The inmate "grievance clerk" and the guard-panelist can become constructive and involved colleagues. Their search for fair solutions can serve the mutual goal of reducing staff-inmate conflict. This aim, like the mission of the police peer review panelists referred to earlier, can defeat pro-violence norms. It can inspire new concerns centered on equity, openness, collaboration, empathy, and insight.

But the model is limited because it is specialized. Although rotating membership may spread some effect, the impact is confined to the actual inmate and staff participants. The bulk of staff and inmates continue to labor under prevailing conflict norms.

Building Problem Solving into Subcultures

J.D. Grant recently pointed out that "subcultures of both inmates and correc-tional officers can be developed to be supportive forces in handling their shared problems of coexistence" [53, p. 188] . This statement refers to the possibility of generalizing participation, from grievance-handling to other ways of insuring that "officers in correctional institutions and their clients . . . be effective forces in developing programs for managing conflict" [53, p. 183] .

In discussing police experiments in chapter 3 we suggested that rank-and-file problem solving is a powerful tool for change. Paul Katsampes [68] makes the same point about prison guards, and documents it with an interesting ex-perience in training. The context was a major in-service training program for New York corrections personnel. Experienced officers were used to prepare "problem-solving" materials. These officers constructed vignettes of the kind Ross Flanagan has called "critical incidents": these are real situations that require complex decisions with important consequences. Among guards, many of the incidents featured situations in which force was an option that could have been exercised.

In actual training, the incidents were presented to class members for spontaneous decisions. Groups were formed to discuss individual incidents for "best" solutions. The class then met to discuss group recommendations. Small and large groups proceeded to consider "general principles" involved in responses to the incidents. The incident questionnaires were finally adminis-tered again.

The results were impressive. The officers had become engrossed and ex-cited; they participated animatedly, questioned their own assumptions, considered new options. In their proposed "solutions", shifts occurred toward options considered "constructive." Such shifts held even where subcultural forces entered into the vignettes, such as in the following:

You arrive on duty after two days off and discover an inmate who has a serious bite injury. According to the previous day's report, the inmate was involved in a fight twenty-four hours before you came on duty. The officer on duty during the fight recorded the incident as causing no injuries. The inmate patient wants to know what can be done about his injury, and you must file a report on the reported injury. How would you word this report?

Among responses to this sample item, a decrease occurred in officers who proposed to "cover" for peers; an increase occurred in the full disclosure option [68, p. 37 ff]. In violent or violence-prone incidents, including group confrontations, officers sought nonviolent moves, and exercised ingenuity in doing so. New ideas emerged. Of 550 trainees,

only ten officers evaluated the situations as having no impact on their attitudes. . . . In evaluation forms, the officers classified group discussions as the most influential category (of their in-service training program) and lecture classes (the bulk of their training) as the lowest [68, p. 59].

New Guard Roles

Occasionally guards are placed in nontraditional, noncustodial roles. They generally respond with high participation, increased morale, and sophisticated performances.

A personal experience is relevant. It involves a psychiatric prison in which the superintendent (a psychiatrist) knew of excessive force by guards. Civil service procedures and a militant union precluded countermeasures. In group meetings, the officers proved bitter, alienated and cynical. Labor–management negotiations degenerated into acrimonious name calling.

A number of program shifts resulted in a reorganized institution, in which inmates were grouped into "therapeutic milieus" (see chapter 7). Each unit or "center" had its own custodial force. Guards participated in unit meetings, and those guards who were interested (more than half the force) carried case loads of inmates for "counselling." This involved individual and group encounters, crisis intervention, and referral functions. Mental health personnel were teamed with guards. The officers were accepted, respected as partners, and visibly appreciated.

The programs developed a new esprit de corps. Cynical officers found fresh meaning in their work. They related with friendliness and humor to inmates, and to administrators. The guards became concerned with "their" inmates, with the inmates' efforts to cope, and with their postprison prospects.

The positive concern was reciprocated by inmates, who proved loyal and grateful to guards.

The story anticlimaxed. Therapy programs were transferred, and inmates were shifted elsewhere. The guards had substantial job worries, but they seemed most concerned about the fate of "their" programs and "their" charges. Inmates were panicked, but *mostly about their separation from officers.* Petitions were filed. A community (now ruptured) had formed.

Changes in officer functions lead to changes in inmates. As roles are broadened, new relationships form. Links develop between clients and staff which undermine adversary or countercultures. Strained poses are dropped or attenuated. Clients permit themselves to trust, respect, talk, and listen. They are open to "social learning."

Briggs and Dowling [23] document social learning in guards trained as "consultants." They report tangible shifts from (1) "officers (who) seemed to maintain their traditional roles rather rigidly," to (2) officers as observers of inmate behavior, (3) a sharing of custodial functions, (4) increased concern for inmate motives and group conduct, and (5) "blending of the roles of inmates, officers and counselors" [23, p. 31].

Briggs and Dowling [23] discuss an outcome

which is perhaps most promising and exciting of all, that these particular officers are showing increasing ability to conceptualize some of the very complex situations occurring around them and are able to come forth with impressive creative thinking in situations which would normally induce a great deal of anxiety. (p. 31)

The implication is that where men are locked into "screw-convict" games, the accuracy of their perception and the appropriateness of their conduct are inhibited. Where violence results from clumsiness and miscues, one can try to reduce it through expanded roles.

Officer role expansion (toward counseling) is by now an accepted idea. Glaser [52], among others, records a trend toward guard membership in "treatment teams" and guard involvement as "casework aides" (pp. 206, 210). Officers often run "groups" or formally or informally "counsel." Unfortunately, such activity is sometimes ambiguously defined, and can be a pragmatic promotional gambit where transfer from custodial to mental health job ladders is possible. Nonetheless, counseling work by guards is an intervention with organizational impact where the intervention is substantial and serious enough to pay dividends.

New Inmate Roles

Expanding inmate roles is a familiar notion to wardens. Glaser [52] reminds us that in 1860 Brockway organized convict self-government at the Detroit House of Corrections, and that "junior republics" for delinquents were founded in 1895. Two New York state prisons had inmate "republics" by 1914. Several pioneer prison reformers organized experiments in inmate democracy; one was "Tom Brown" Osborne, who, among other things, ran a guard-free honors camp. Gill, the superintendent of the Norfolk Colony, built a prison with convict help. In 1929, three of Gill's inmates escaped, and inmate-guard teams were instituted:

> The State Police were called in to throw a guard around the place; the men lost much of their freedom and were compelled to spend their free time mostly in the houses. Mr. Gill in a mass meeting put the problem up to the men. As probably never before in the history of prison government, an inmate got up in the meeting and asked Mr. Gill whether he would be willing to sit down with the representatives from the houses in order to discover some plan that would reclaim the privileges lost to them through the recent escapes. The council system, agreeing to share officially in the safety and security of Norfolk, thus had its earliest beginning. Two men from each house were elected to the council. The council kept an eye on suspects, reported to the administration those who could not be dissuaded from intending to escape, inspected the houses for contraband, and even suggested to the staff likely candidates from Charlestown whom they knew personally.
>
> After another escape, the council went further and recommended an inmate watch to be maintained at all hours, night and day, when the men were not under the direct supervision of the staff [43, p. 83].

A problem with inmate organizations is the ascendency, in many convict councils, of subcultural norms. The most frequent way in which this occurs is through the domination of councils by inmate "politicians" or "Big Shots." Glaser [52] notes that "in several institutions corrupt inmates got control of the self-government and used it for their purposes" (p. 218). The councils may also become unrepresentatively militant. In Norfolk, for example,

> as the colony grew the council became less and less co-operative and seemed to develop into a "chiselling body". . . . The council, once a live and enthusiastic body working jointly with the staff in the maintenance of the institution, became an antagonistic, grumbling body. It could have served the staff well as an index to the growing dissatisfaction of the inmates but the majority of the staff failed to take note of it in this manner. . . . Inmate participation and co-operation, at first high, gradually and then more rapidly disappeared until finally antagonism replaced it [43, p. 8].

The second trend—often a reaction to the first—is that of the staff "takeover." This occurs where inmate councils are emasculated, or where contaminated appointments create transparent "fink groups." Inmate participation may be confined to ridiculous trivia. In many prisons, for instance, the juiciest agenda item for inmate self-government is the film series or the baseball schedule.

Similar problems befall the time-honored prison-inmate teacher. At best, such men are inmates with cushy jobs. At worst, they become pawns of peers. Glaser [52] reports that

men who had been assigned to school teaching in the penitentiaries told of the pressure from inmates to give good grades, to allow cheating on assignments or tests, and to let class discussions wander for indefinite periods to sports, crime, or other topics irrelevant to the assigned study topic. The inmate teachers who balked at this were subject to reprisal from other inmates, while the inmate teachers who complied might expect reciprocal favors, and had a "soft job" in which they were considered "right guys." (pp. 268–69).

Such facts need not blind us to what is possible. Inmate suicide aides and inmate counselors have emerged in some settings. Suicide aides watch for symptoms of depression in jail inmates, and counselors deal with day-to-day coping problems. Although the performance of such inmates may be marginal at times (e.g., "if you hurt yourself, I'll clobber you" or "let me tell you what I did"), there is potential in these programs, with improved selection and training, for decreasing the coldness of prison climates and for giving isolated inmates an opportunity to relate significantly to others. Crisis managers and conflict reducers are other new options; they are in use (in California), for preventing gang or group conflicts among violence-prone men in "readjustment" settings. Other new roles are inmate subculture linkers (for Latin inmates), and convict members of mental health teams [175].

Prison Communities

A more systemic intervention involves the creation of new forms of inmate-staff organization in which subcultural norms are neutralized with a sense of community, of fairness, and of responsibility for others [154, 185]. The achievement of staff-inmate community in prisons can affect institutional violence levels, since the prime subcultural contribution to violence is the protection and insulation of aggression.

A powerful protagonist of staff-inmate models was the Soviet educator A.S. Makarenko. In his Gorky Colony (1920) and in collectives for delinquent orphans, Makarenko ran institutions along "Swiss" democratic lines. In his epic *The Road to Life* [78] Makarenko recounts a variety of incidents in which violence was at issue. The following exchange, which occurred in a heated free-for-all, is typical:

"You're a Gorkyite now," I told him. "You must learn to respect your comrades. You won't bully the little ones anymore, will you?"
Khovrakh blinked gravely, and indicated a smile with the merest flicker of

his lower lip. There had been more threat than tenderness in my question, and I could see that Khovrakh had made a note of this fact. His reply was brief:

"All right!"

"Not all right, but 'very good,' confound you!" rang out Belukhin's powerful tenor.

Without the slightest ceremony Matvei swung Khovrakh round by the shoulders, smote him simultaneously on each drooping hand, one of which he deftly lifted in a salute, at the same time dropping out, word by word:

"Very good—no bullying the little ones! Now *you* say it!" [78, vol. 3, p. 96].

The best-known contemporary staff–inmate experiment is the Niantic Project at the Connecticut State Farm for Women. The setting is one in which "there had been a near-riot . . . and feelings between staff and inmates were generally hostile" [154, p. 8]. In this climate, an effort was made to set up a joint "constitutional convention" for staff and inmates, which was charged with the task of drafting a rule structure for the institution.

McLeery [84] notes that the opening up of inmate staff communications may be harder for inmates than for officers: "Any attrition of the ideal that the good convict never 'talks to a screw'," he writes, "tends to remove a vital conceptual basis for social hierarchy in inmate society" (p. 175). At Niantic, Scharf and Kohlberg encountered resistance from all factions, but the most obdurate difficulty proved to be inmate resistance to violations of peer solidarity. Scharf and Kohlberg [154] illustrate the problem, and its solution, in the following account:

One inmate said bluntly in one of the first meetings, "I'll do anything you like in this program, I'll talk in groups. The only thing I won't do is lock or rat out one of my sisters."

After a long series of meetings in which inmates successfully "covered-up" for other inmates who had committed minor offenses, the women began to see that if they didn't maintain the rules, the cottage would plunge toward anarchy and the project fail. The crisis came in a meeting in which an inmate named Melinda announced that if anyone brought up her name, she would "stomp their heads in with her boot." After a long hush, the same woman who had announced that she would not punish another inmate stood up and said:

"Melinda, if we let you go around saying you're gonna stomp people, we are gonna lose all respect for this house, the cottage and ourselves. We are going to punish you not to hurt you, but to keep respect." (p. 10)

Staff–inmate community models seem promising, because (1) they permit the functional interconnectedness of inmate and staff to emerge, which cannot happen where we create treatment-oriented staff among treatment-resistant inmates [84], or where we increase client expectations that are doomed of fulfillment; (2) these models also provide norms: they do not place progressive inmates or staff in setting in which they can only elect to defend or betray peers in structurally ordained class struggles. Peaceful resolutions can be best arrived at where ethical norms may be negotiated and shared.

Where the aim is to "solve" interpersonal and organizational problems nonviolently, one must create a problem-solving milieu. This ideally means a climate, among staff and inmates, where violence is a last, despised resort. It means a climate where violence never yields a manly self-image and peer prestige, but where it denotes the failure, clumsiness, or capitulation that it really represents.

6 The "Dangerous" Inmate

Issues of personality arise with violence chronicity. Most people, including police and prison staff, see repeat aggressors as dangerous persons rather than as actors in discrete incidents. This perspective seems particularly germane when it comes to protecting the public. Criminal justice agencies are presumed to secure the rest of us from violent onslaughts by violent clients. This charge implies the obligation to defuse or neutralize men who are violence prone.

There is a suspicion in the public mind that one can tell beforehand whether a person will be violent in the future, particularly when he becomes *very* violent. This seems to follow from the fact that *once we know* that a person was violent, we can hunt and find clues in his past. One forgets that we do this by interpreting biographical data in the light of what we *now know*. If the same person were a pacifist we could just as well select information to explain his nonviolence.

In a recent incident in upstate New York, a high school senior went on a sniping spree, and killed three persons. As often occurs in such cases, the youth was a model student, friendly, gentle, hard working, concerned with religious activities and involved with his studies and hobbies. His acquaintances were nonplussed. A teacher confessed to the *New York Times* that

I kept asking myself, was there something in his behavior I missed . . . and the answer kept coming back—nothing, nothing, nothing. I know it sounds like a cliché—a perfect student, kind and considerate, an altar boy—but it's all true. There never was a clue of a problem. He was brilliant, self-possessed and considerate [132].

Fortunately, the boy had a hobby that seemed relevant. The *Times* headline, "Sniper's Classmate Says Guns were 'Whole Life'" draws attention to an interest the boy had displayed in target shooting. And it sounds plausible that if the young man's passion had been stamp collecting, his crisis might have taken a different turn. But diagnosis is not prediction. Most boys involved in rifle clubs kill no one. And even if the boy's guns make some of us queasy, we have other information about him ("perfect student, kind and considerate," etc.) that does not make a case against him.

Postdiction is easy, because *in one essential* respect it is infallible; no matter how far-fetched our explanation, the outcome is given. Even if we traced a boy's sniping to his sterling character, there would be no chance of error.[a] The fact

---

[a]One type of violence-prone person tends to be milder and less assertive than others. He controls himself so rigidly that his explosions, if or when they occur, are extreme [86].

that the individual did act violently makes the presumption safe that anything about him has some bearing on his violence. The point remains that all our information lapses into insignificance if our subject has not become violent. No one maintains that we must watch model students who enjoy hunting for latent murderous tendencies. The predictive value of our post hoc explanations—however ingenious—is nil.[b]

Although most people would grant this argument for choir-boys-turned-snipers, their view changes when (1) a violent act is committed by a person who has engaged in violence before, and (2) the person has been a client of a mental health or criminal justice agency. In such cases, the presumption is virtually universal that any fool should have known that violence was inevitable, and that professional staff (who are experts) were duty bound to predict it. The following *New York Times* headlines are typical of this presumption:

PAROLEE IS GUILTY OF BRUTAL SLAYING
Convicted in Bronx of Fatal Beating of Woman, 75, 5 Weeks after Release [131]

MENTAL PATIENT KILLED IN PLUNGE
Bronx State Inmate Had Set 2nd Fire in His Room—Merola Begins Inquiry [128]

SEX-SLAYING CASE INVOLVING A "MODEL INMATE" IS RAISING QUESTIONS FOR THE STATE'S CRIMINAL JUSTICE SYSTEM [126]

SUSPECT IN BEAUTY-SHOP RAPE IS SEIZED IN A 2D, SIMILAR CASE [125]

SLAYING SUSPECT WAS "GOOD RISK"
Parole Board Cites Record—Held in "Village" Murder [124]

DOCTORS' DECISION ALLOWED SUSPECT'S RELEASE IN JULY [120]

TRUSTY GIVES UP IN JERSEY MURDER
Serving Manslaughter Term, He was Out of Prison on a Weekend Furlough [113]

It is obvious from the reaction of sophisticated journalistic observers that if a criminal justice client repeats a violent offense, his act suggests staff negligence. Since the man's prior offense helps to explain the subsequent one, we assume that the man's "dangerousness" was implied by his first crime.

Statistically, this presumption is false. Three-year follow-ups of parolees across the country tell us, for instance, that only 1 percent of men imprisoned for homicide commit a new murder and only 1 percent of paroled rapists rape again.[c] The recidivism rates for violent offenders (other than armed robbers) are much lower than those for other offenders.

---

[b]The *New York Times,* in summarizing the 127th meeting on the American Psychiatric Association, relates that "doctor after doctor said at the convention here that it was impossible to diagnose or predict 'dangerousness' with any degree of assurance, *given an absence of previous violent acts"* [119, italics added]. However, even when a history of previous violent acts does exist, the prediction of further violence involves tremendously high rates of false positives [189].

[c]These figures derive from the three-year follow-up and analysis of 1969 parolees published

It is true that one could prevent *some* murders and rapes by refusing to parole all men convicted of such offenses. But as a consequence of this strategy, 99 persons would have been erroneously detained (as "false positives") to neutralize one individual who would repeat his offense.

Searching for the "Violent Personality"

But all murderers and rapists may not be equally dangerous, and we could concentrate on locating the most clearly ominous specimens. It stands to reason that the one-in-a-hundred repeater must have personality traits or motives different from those of offenders who do not repeat. Accordingly, it should be possible to pinpoint such traits, and to sort the "dangerous offender," who has them, from the "nondangerous" offender, who does not.

The first problem with this way of thinking lies in the fact that the "trait" picture does not apply to violence. Personality must interact with situations for behavior to occur, and interactions are hard to predict. It is possible, for example, that a propensity toward jealousy may relate to violence. But for violence to occur, a man must be faced with a presumption of unfaithfulness. If we detained all jealous murderers, we might improve our "batting average," but we might, equally well, make it worse. For not one of the men we detain might have encountered a situation that could provoke him to violence, while some of our "controls" (whoever they are) could become messily involved.

The second problem relates to the artificiality of our tests. A burglar who rapes middle-aged women may be a shy, retiring citizen. More relevantly, he may be the Milquetoast of the prison yard. Yet the same man may explode with suppressed desire (or with rage) when entering a window. Where a man reacts with violence when he is drunk, prisons cannot determine (a) that the man is permanently on the wagon, or (b) that he has overcome his belligerent-drunk routine if he drinks. This holds particularly where the incriminating pattern is clear to the offender, and helps him stage demonstrations (such as AA membership) of reform.

In a New York case, a sex strangler committed in 1966 was convicted of an identical crime in 1974, after his release. The superintendent of the prison pointed out that the man "was the classic version of the rehabilitation system working at its best. . . . He became a model inmate who seemed to have learned his lesson . . . he did everything, and more than was asked of him." The prison psychiatrist tells us that the man "was rehabilitated and one of the best, brightest, most articulate prisoners I have ever seen" [126]. A New Jersey inmate who axed a man while on furlough was described as a superlative risk. A correctional official, after reviewing the man's file, reported that "he fit the standards for work release and if it came up again tomorrow he'd be released again" [113].

---

by the Uniform Parole Reports in October, 1974. The findings are consistent with data previously summarized by National Parole Reports.

A third difficulty relates to the uniqueness of links (if any) between mental states and violence [156]. There is no syndrome or diagnostic category that describes mental patients with violence problems or violent persons who are emotionally disturbed [136]. And if we do have a clear instance of illness linked to violence, the clarity of the syndrome does not translate into ease of prediction. Remission of psychosis in prison is not a guarantee that a man will not break down when faced with complexities in life. But even where psychosis is present, it need nevermore take explosive shape. Bernard Rubin [149], who reviewed the cases of 17 offenders incarcerated as dangerous and mentally ill, concluded that "of the 17, one may have been dangerous on release because of the inaccessibility and catatonic features of his psychosis. . . . He was the only possibility in that category" (p. 405). Follow-up studies of two very large groups of men diagnosed as "dangerously mentally ill" showed that few of these men proved "dangerous" when released by court order [166; 167; 173; 192], although many did stay ill.

The artificiality of institutional tests of dangerousness cuts both ways. On the one hand, model inmates may prove to be killers outside prison. On the other hand, fights in the prison yard may be no index of how a man handles himself in his living room. Conflict situations in prisons are products of social pressures and social situations that most ex-inmates are unlikely to encounter in real life. The California studies we have referred to show that by far the best predictor of prison violence is past prison violence. The same point is made by Tong and MacKay [180] for men incarcerated in a maximum security hospital, and by Halfon and Steadman [56] for female patients.

Beefing up the Statistics

There are those who believe that we can forecast violence by starting with the one predictive fact we know about (past violence) and searching for other such facts, without worrying about "making sense" of the violent person. This strategy is called the "empirical" approach to prediction. Instead of trying to describe what violent men are like, it seeks to locate "associated" factors that may occur more frequently where we find violence. By juggling such factors in combination, one seeks to assign probabilities to violent recidivism. Should this strategy work, we could learn to distinguish *statistically* between men who have engaged in violence but are unlikely to do so again, and those men who, having been violent, have a chance of repeating their conduct.

But even the highest statistical "risk" groups of violent offenders turn out to have no more than a slight chance of recidivism. No matter what predictors we add to any "dangerousness" equation, most violence candidates stubbornly remain slated for nonviolent careers.

Wenk *et al* [189] cite a very carefully done California study that attempted to predict parole violence. After considerable statistical effort a group was isolated,

14 percent of whom could be expected to violate parole by a violent or potentially violent discovered act. This likelihood was nearly three times as great as that for parolees in general, whose violence probability, by the same criterion, was only 5 percent. (p. 395)

If we forced treatment on this "high risk" group, six nonviolent clients would be processed for every real risk. And given the small number of risk candidates, which gets smaller as we add predictors to give power to the prediction, only a small fraction of violence can be prevented this way.

In violence prevention, the odds are always against us. Most violence is committed by men who have not been previously violent, which is the group for whom we cannot predict at all. Of those who have been violent, only a small number become violent again. This unpromising ratio is the "base-rate" problem deplored in the violence-prediction literature.

We know that a small group of recidivists are violent very often, and account for a disproportionate share of violence. But this fact is useless for prevention programs; by the time we locate such men with confidence, it is usually too late. They will tend to have done their deeds; and their time behind bars extends, usually, beyond their violence-prone years.

Statistics are poor guides for those who decide the fate of individual men. The decision maker cannot readily use statements such as "this man has a 23 percent probability of becoming violent." To hold or release a flesh-and-blood individual, the premise must be that "this man is dangerous" or that "he is not." One likes to feel that one's judgments are made on the basis of assessments of personal attributes, no matter how stereotypical or "classic" a statistical syndrome sits across the table.

Violence Prediction in Practice

Statements about inmate dangerousness in classification usually involve impressionistic judgments by correctional administrators. Men are placed in maximum security settings, for example, on the basis of a staff member's sense of alarm, derived from the inmate's aggressive demeanor or disciplinary record. Since decisions can be made by invoking past conduct (which justifies punishment) there is no pressure to specify the diagnostic or prognostic reasoning on the basis of which extra time, more severe placement, or additional security are allotted.

The most explicit judgments about violence potential in corrections are made by psychiatrists, who make them at a number of decision points. As one group of psychiatrists pointed out, "according to virtually all dangerous persons legislation, an individual cannot be legally identified as dangerous until psychiatry has diagnosed him as such" [71, p. 374].[d]

Given the widespread role of psychiatry, the decision process of psychiatrists is illuminating. In practice, as noted by Steadman [164; 165], the pressure for psychiatrists to "overpredict" is enormous. While the released rapist inspires a storm of protest, the constituency of the detained murderer (however unnecessarily detained) is negligible. Understandably, psychiatrists accommodate a large number of *false positives*—persons classified as violent who would not become violent—to avoid the chance of any *false negatives*—persons released who later do become violent. False negatives makes news, where false positives are never heard from again. Steadman [164] points to two other propensities of psychiatrists charged with adjudging dangerousness. The first of these is a tendency to invoke vague or circular justification (like referring to a man's "propensity to act out") when a rationale for their decisions is asked for. A more important issue arises where psychiatrists rely—as most do—on their subject's alleged commitment offense. This factor happens to be available to judges and administrators, who have the grace not to build on it themselves.

Beyond past violence, the so-called "clinical" criteria sometimes used by psychiatrists may describe individuals who are distasteful, immature, obnoxious, and uncongenial.[e] This "syndrome" is hard to divorce from the psychiatrist's dealings with the patient, and we are reminded of Steadman's warning that "dangerousness is in the eyes of the beholder." Kozol and his colleagues [71] furnish an example of this problem, when they tell us that:

We conceived of the dangerous person as one who has actually inflicted or attempted to inflict serious physical injury on another person; harbors anger, hostility, and resentment; enjoys witnessing or inflicting suffering; lacks altruistic and compassionate concern for others; sees himself as a victim rather than as an aggressor; resents or rejects authority; is primarily concerned with his own satisfaction and with the relief of his own discomfort; is intolerant of frustration or delay of satisfaction; lacks control of his own impulses; has immature attitudes toward social responsibility; lacks insight into his own psychological structure; and distorts his perception of reality in accordance with his own wishes and needs. (p. 379)

---

[d]It is ironic that another group of psychiatrists concludes that "neither psychiatrists nor anyone else have reliably demonstrated an ability to predict future violence or 'dangerousness.' Neither has any special psychiatric 'expertise' in this area been established" [4, p. 28].

[e]Steadman's data suggest that standard psychotic symptoms (most notably, delusional thinking) are sometimes invoked by psychiatrists. This fact is troublesome, because mental illness and dangerousness are separate and different categories. It is to determine *which* psychotic reactions *functionally* relate to *future* violence that expertise is invoked. No one understands psychosis well enough to extrapolate future conduct from distortions of a patient's reality world. The proportion of schizophrenics with delusional systems (even blood-thirsty delusions) who commit new violent acts is probably lower than that of nonpsychotic offenders.

The Transactional Nature of Dangerousness

Webster's Dictionary informs us that *dangerous* implies "trouble making" and "hard to please"; one connotation is "involving risk, demanding caution or care as extremely unsafe," and another is "able or likely to inflict injury; causing or threatening harm." The dictionary also points out that the word "dangerous" applies to "persons or things to be avoided or treated carefully as generally unsafe and likely to cause or be attended by danger."

The generic meaning is transactional in character: one must "make trouble" for *someone*. "Trouble" involves a person who is "distressed, annoyed, or perturbed"; a *trouble maker* is a man who "causes friction."

"Hard to please" implies that one is being "pleased" or displeased. "Caution or care" are attributes of classifiers, which may be "demanded" by their feelings as well as by threats in the world. The "ability" to inflict harm is a capacity of the person being judged; there is no implication that such a skill will be deployed. And "likelihood" is an unverifiable judgment made now about the future.

The assessment of whether a person is "to be avoided or treated carefully" depends on the avoider or treater. Some individuals are characterized by timidity, others by foolhardiness. A man in fear will "avoid or treat carefully" a large number of people (who become "dangers"). On the other end of the spectrum, self-confidence provides an illusion of imperviousness.

It is obvious that when we are faced with categorizations of "dangerousness" and "nondangerousness" we must know as much (or more) about the persons making the judgment as about the person being judged. "Dangerousness" is a product of stimulus characteristics and rater attributes, containing an unknown proportion of each. While we explore the former, we usually deny that the latter exists. This makes it hard to systematize or to objectify the premises and reactions of classifiers.

Leslie Wilkins suggests (probably tongue-in-cheek) that "moral trade-offs" involving judgments of "moral acceptability," be included in the classification of dangerousness [193]. A man with six violent acts could be viewed as less meritorious than a one-time offender; a heinous crime could detract from one's right to freedom. No scientific excuse need be made for increased hard-nosedness in classifying persons whose past conduct is more reprehensible or unpalatable. The rater becomes more willing to buy false positives as the client looks less deserving.

Such a proposal has the virtue of honesty. It circumvents the pretense of diagnosing or predicting where the real variables lie in social perception. We do not have to talk of "strong impulses and weak controls" when we encounter callousness, nor do we have to describe a cruel person as "sociopathic" or as a "character disorder." The client's uncontrollability or nuisance value can be explicitly faced, rather than being left for others to infer later. Even alert newspaper readers know that in corrections the "dangerous offender" is a product of decision-maker bias. We read approvingly in the *New York Times* that

the city is rushing a program to remove all teenaged children from the Children's Center . . . where gangs of adolescent girls have terrorized other children and the staff and where rape, arson, and thievery are frequent occurrences [127].

Turning to the editorial page on another occasion, we are informed to our chagrin that:

Inmate "trouble-makers" are often those first "selected" for (behavior modification) programs, for obvious reasons; yet, the trouble-maker is often the most independent and tough-minded prisoner, in rebellion against lock-step treatment . . . behavior modification smacks of extra punishment . . . handed out for the convenience of prison administrators [118].

One fact emerging from the literature is that it is very hard to differentiate behavior and attitudes from each other. In a study of riot assaulters Skelton [159] notes that "the descriptive phrase 'resentful of authority' had frequently been applied to these inmates" (p. 362). In another study of prison rioters, Grosz, Stern and Feldman [54] point out that

in the institution, prior to the riot, the staff generally characterized the non-rioters as cooperative, fearful and conforming to the institution's rules and regulations and the rioters generally as uncooperative, hostile, defiant, aggressive, impulsive and violent. (p. 1378)

Such judgments are correlated with test summaries and clinical ratings, which—although they are represented as "objective," are susceptible to contamination through interpretations.[f] Skelton's [159] observation, for example, that "14 (82.3%) of the assaulters had been identified as disturbed" (p. 361), relays impressions by mental health staff that are no different in kind from custodial evaluations.

Staff perceptions of "dangerousness" are influenced by inmate views of staff. Skelton's [159] label "resentment of authority" derives from the fact that "the inmate was scored as resentful of authority when the record contains comments such as 'sullen when given instructions,' 'hostile to staff,' 'makes verbal threats when given instructions,' or 'insolent at times'" (p. 360). The picture is one of *inter*personal hostility, and it is difficult to assign primacy to inmates or staff in such cycles.

But what if the data suggest that "dangerous inmates" tend to have records

---

[f]Grosz *et al.* [54], for instance, reproduce scores for the High School Personality Profile. The two negative items on which rioters excel are "expedient, evades rules, feels few obligations," and "undisciplined self-conflict, follows own urges, careless of protocol."

of violent offenses, as has been reported for prison rioters [54, 159]? We are dealing here with group or subcultural conflicts. In such situations, we have seen that individuals are often assigned militant roles by peers. Such roles are most likely to fall upon the shoulders of men who are seen as specially tough. The opposition may also single out violence-experienced men for observation. If a riot featured a blood-thirsty chaplain and a peace-loving chief guard, reconstructions of staff roles would probably center on the custodial officer.

Labeled violent offenders are cautiously dealt with in classifications and other staff actions. Some inmates (old-line lifers) prove the inapplicability of stereotypes that are based on offenses. But some violent offenders react to staff in ways that confirm and accelerate staff concern. Moreover, security classifications physically group tough inmates, and we have noted that this increases the chances of violence. By ignorantly combining the wrong persons with each other a situation can be devised so that the meekest inmates (faced with the need to make a last stand) will attack their suspected aggressors; and psychotics may be driven to explosion by increasing social overstimulation or pressure. Background variables relate to types of violence promoted by types of situations, which includes the way people are labelled, assigned, and intermixed.

Where labels translate into sanctions, where they are passed on and form the basis of other labels, where they are incorporated into reputations and favorable self-images, they enhance dangerousness. If a man is dubbed a "psychopath," is deemed a "trouble maker" and is secreted in special housing among the inmate elite, his chance of living down the combined honor and stigma are slim. By contrast, verbal categorizing, with no social consequences, is not violence producing.

The distinction is supported by Adrian Cheatwood's [30] study of boys officially labeled dangerous in the Ohio correctional system for youths. These boys carried identification numbers (publicly known) with the suffix "R" or "E". This suffix was

designed to identify those youth, who in the opinion of the staff member, "may be considered as dangerous or potentially dangerous to the community or to themselves." Generally, this is interpreted to mean those boys who are hostile or aggressive. (p. 1)

The purpose of the suffix was to reflect the classifier's premise that the offender could become an embarrassment to the organization by committing a violent offense following his release. The label was then ignored. Cheatwood quotes one staff member as testifying that "nothing at all special happens to the 'R's' and 'E's' " (p. 29).

Cheatwood tells us that "for the staff member, the "R" and "E" boy is basically the same as the non-"R" and "E" boy in terms of characteristics, and if staff members' assessments are valid, he is generally treated in the same manner" (pp. 68–69). As a result of this tendency, the suffixed inmates merged into the population; they were viewed by peers as somewhat "tougher" than average, but not enough to modify the boy's conduct.

Self-fulfilling Prophecies and Nonprophecies

Cheatwood's finding is worth mention because it draws our attention away from verbal labels, which are viewed as evil by some sociologists, and points us at the uses, or nonuses, of labels. Even where violent offenders are not dealt with, as in Wilkins' scheme, on the basis of their reprehensibility, classifications of dangerousness tell us as much about the users of classification schemes as about the objects of classification. They tell us about the games that are played in prisons between and among staff and offenders.

Given the current state of the art, we cannot set aside violence-prone persons; what we can do is set aside persons we wish to set aside, under color of violence proneness. Ultimately it does not matter whether targets of classification are selected clinically and personally, or by lot. Even statistically, we spawn interactions between some staff and some men who have been designated worthy or overwhelming adversaries. Where "dangerous" inmates pick up the gauntlet, there is "documentation" for the warfare model of corrections, there are threats to titillate danger glands, and role models or norms for machismo.

Given such pay-off, we are tempted to classify more eagerly than the facts justify. The enthusiasm with which the game is played makes us forget the ostensible object of the game. Those who are classified, no matter how pitiful they may be, become tough, fearsome, potent, and vicious. They become all-purpose proving grounds for staff manliness, and (more often than not) for their own.

Goals of Classification

If classification were done to some advantage, it would have several uses, which can be distinguished from each other. One such use is for treatment. The appropriate data here relate to needs for services the person has that can be met by available treatment strategies. Violent behavior is relevant only as a cue to (or a symptom of) personal difficulties that we can help to address. One expects personal difficulties to include commodities such as poor interpersonal skills, incongruent or strained playing of roles, and low self-esteem. Problems of this kind relate to violence, but are shared by inmates who are violence prone and others who are not.

The second purpose, which must not be confused with the first, is to emphasize the seriousness or gruesomeness of a man's past conduct. The purpose of such a classification would be to alert releasing authorities to the embarrassment of potentially inflammatory false negatives. The point here would be to attach a "red flag" suffix, which (as in Cheatwood's sample) should convey *no implication at all* for the way we perceive or treat the man in prison.

The third grouping could denote men who through conduct consisting of *violent behavior in the institution* become threats to other inmates and to staff. Such men must not be confused with a diagnostic group, nor with the clientele for treatment programs. They can be regarded as extreme management and classification problems. In their case, the task is of finding *or creating* special milieus in which (a) the chances of victimization of others is reduced, and (b) violence as a prison adjustment mode can be dealt with, to insure early reintegration of the inmate into the larger inmate community.[g] Models for such an enterprise may not currently exist, but we shall explore relevant possibilities later.

The fourth grouping (not to be confused with the former) is of inmates who have difficulties relating to staff, and of staff who have problems with inmates. The category involved here is of *interpersonal* conflicts. These may comprise all sorts of grievances, from legitimate, substantive complaints to pseudo issues that derive from degenerating encounters and polarization. The programmatic implications of such grouping lie in conflict reduction and problem solving. Although ready-made tools in this area are few, we shall also discuss one or two of the relevant options that come to mind.

Classification can finally aid the improvement of knowledge. This entails separating out persons whose violence experience is roughly comparable. With the help of such persons, we can embark on research designed to address the vacuum in our knowledge about violence. This is probably the most crucial classification goal of all. For until we know more about violence, we can expect to encounter difficulties in our attempts to classify violent men, to predict their future conduct, and to address their concerns.

---

[g]It is similarly possible to think of grouping chronic inmate victims, with a view to building up their interpersonal skills and teaching them strategies to neutralize the risk of being victimized. There are also advantages, as Wolfgang points out, to systematic monitored intermixing of offenders. "By conscious design," according to Wolfgang [195], "proper blending of small numbers of violent inmates with non-violent ones could result in the latter's promoting values of nonviolence through ... social interaction" (pp. 123-24).

7 Treatment for Violent Inmates

Few issues in criminal justice arise with as much heat as the question of what prisons should do to (or for) violent offenders.

The public demands that rapists and muggers be "dealt with," and in some cases, the import of this mandate is very clear. If a man is a cold-blooded callous offender, we are told to lock him up and to throw away the key. But if the man shows signs of bizarreness, we are expected to "treat" him so as to "cure" him. If the man is both bizarre and callous, we must "cure" him, take our time about it, and throw away the key.

When prisons respond to these public demands, some lawyers object to "compulsory" programming, some critics equate treatment with torture, and some scientists stress difficulties in providing effective treatment and in demonstrating change. Prison therapists find themselves accused of engaging in unconstitutional exercises of barbarism under totalitarian auspices against helpless men, who (paradoxically) are unaffected.

The least controversial sort of treatment program is one that reassures people that violence-prone offenders will remain locked up, while it also reassures them that no one's rights are being tampered with. Such a program tries to locate basically safe persons and makes the most convincing possible case for their release. While it helps safe men get out of prison, it leaves others (those who are not safe) unimpeded.

One intervention that was defined in such terms is the Stress Assessment Unit established in October 1962 at the California Medical Facility (a prison) in Vacaville. This program deals exclusively with clients who have been labeled "violent and bizarre" by the parole board and who have little chance of obtaining freedom except by going through the program. The purpose of the program is not to change the violent inmate, but to try to assess his explosiveness, and to facilitate parole for the inmate if he seems able to handle himself. Treatment is reserved for the man who returns to the community, and is designed to ease the transition.

The Stress Assessment (SA) Unit evolved informally over time. It aimed at the construction of environments analogous to structured and democratic community situations that could provoke aggressive responses from violence-prone men. In the words of ex-director Heise,

the design of the total program is such that the stresses inherent in real life situations are used and intensified as a means to evaluate inmates whose past

93

reactions to situational stress has, in many instances, resulted in violent or bizarre behavior [58, p. 3].

This argument holds, of course, only as long as the "stresses" in the program replicate problems that a released inmate is likely to encounter, later. Tests cannot be disproportionate, nor excessively severe. Unfortunately there is no "calculus of stress," which makes such a determination possible. There is also the general difficulty of the negative image of "stress." Jessica Mitford [92], who typifies radical critics of correctional treatment, summarizes the SA program (in a chapter called "Clockwork Orange") by telling us that

the prisoner lives in an open dormitory where it is expected he will suffer maximum irritation from the lack of privacy. He is assigned to the worst and most menial jobs. In compulsory group therapy sessions staff members deliberately bait the men and try to provoke conflicts among them. The idea is to see how much of this a person can stand without losing his temper. (pp. 126-27)

The "compulsory sessions" referred to by Mitford are the unit's community meetings, which featured a good deal of frank talk about "here and now" living problems, which could (and did) include personal conflicts. The "stress" did not lie in "deliberate baiting," but in tempting the inmates to abandon their game playing and defenses by participating in open discussions and in the making of program decisions. Such participation is not easy for men who feel comfortable with conventional ways of doing time; but this does not mean that anyone's personal integrity is violated.

It is hard to visualize tests of violence proneness that would not entail some stress. Men do not explode while they walk in the sunshine plucking daisies; wolves look lamb-like if they are not hungry or tempted; selfish men ooze charm when the world responds to their requirements. But stress is not the core of an assessment program, any more than final examinations are the soul of education. Mitford—as a dispassionate observer—might have taken note that in the last phases of the SA program, intimate staff-inmate links were often forged, which included joint attendance at ball games, staff hosting inmates for dinner at their homes, etc. She might have noted the fact that unit graduates most frequently requested parole under visiting parole officers, even though this meant moving from Los Angeles to Sacramento. She also might have found it odd that alumni of the SA Unit regularly attended the meetings she characterizes as "compulsory."

Incentives for Treatment

There is, needless to say, some "compulsion" in all prison treatment programs. A man's willingness to participate in a program is related to his desire for parole and freedom; his willingness to please staff is tied to staff's gate-keeping function. Model inmates may be manipulators of subtle or transparent staff predilections. Staff nondirectiveness ("do whatever you feel like") may enhance chances of authentic inmate reactions, but may also increase stress and ambiguity ("what does he want me to do?"). And no obvious alternatives exist to ambiguity, except the sort of structure that yields cues to facilitate surface conformity.

The issue of conformity is particularly relevant to the much-publicized treatment program of the Patuxent Institution for "defective delinquents" in Maryland. It is worth reviewing this program in detail, because it helps pose the central issues involved in institutional treatment for violent offenders.

Inmates in Patuxent are under indeterminate sentences, and are released at the recommendation of staff. A sociologist who visited the institution and talked to some inmates reports that their general stance was to "learn what each therapist wanted to hear, what the therapist's 'trip' was, and to be able to tell about those things, and to do it in the right jargon." The sociologist observes that "the real cure is not therapy, it is the indeterminate sentence" [87, p. 38].

Patuxent staff are more sophisticated than most staff, because they readily admit that inmates make concrete efforts to manipulate them. They concur that patients are "motivated" by indeterminate sentences. Boslow and Manne [21] —two Patuxent staff members—argue that

we deem it necessary to provide a wedge or outside motivating force which will stimulate the patient to change. This stimulus is the indeterminate sentence . . . because the indeterminant sentence is always present to reinforce motivation, the pressure on patients to understand their behavior is always present. (p. 26)

The picture is one of patients who would not really care for treatment unless their release from prison were at stake. This conclusion is confirmed by Patuxent's experience with group therapy. According to Boslow et al. [21], inmate resistance was at first

so great that some men preferred disciplinary action, including going into seclusion, rather than attend group meetings. In the meeting themselves . . . being the first to cooperate and talk was considered a dangerous thing, or a violation of inmate social mores. . . . Sometimes when a patient would attempt to talk, other group members would stop him. (pp. 8–9)

By contrast, inmates later began to "clamor" for treatment, in part because

it became clear to all inmates that those who got out were the ones who had at least managed to convince the professional staff that in some way they had benefitted from it. (p. 10)

The indeterminate sentence obviously leads freedom-thirsty inmates to water: the real question revolves around the issue of what (if anything) inmates drink at the treatment well. If inmates "con" staff, indeterminacy promotes surface conformity among clients and hypocrisy or gullibility by staff. But what if staff "con" the inmates?

Mitford [92] alleges that

"individualized treatment" is primarily a device for breaking the convict's will to resist and hounding him into compliance with institution demands, and is thus a means of exerting maximum control over the convict population. The cure will be deemed effective to the degree that the poor/young/brown/black captive appears to have capitulated to his middle-class/white/middle-aged captor, and to have adopted the virtues of subservience to authority, industry, cleanliness, docility. (p. 117)

But it is not self-evident that the stance of inmates who resist treatment is that of mature men who exercise their right not to be brainwashed by racist forces. We have the countercontention that men may resist change that frees them from comfortable self-enslavement. The norms to which recalcitrant inmates respond need not be values they would subserve if they were free of irrational constraints or of pressures from destructive peers.

There are also questions about how compulsory the incentive system really is. An inmate desiring freedom may have "all the negotiating options of a cornered rat" [92, p. 111], but he can still take an interest in programs. It is possible for a man to accept therapy to get out of prison, and to become involved and to profit from it. The premise that men become helplessly brainwashed because they are induced to talk of themselves is implausible, and is flagrantly inconsistent with the same critics' image of inmates who are fully committed idealists and who are determined at all costs to resist their keepers.

In the case of inmates who do *not* respond to the "incentives" of indeterminacy, the charges of critics and the explanations of treaters tend to converge. Mitford's book alleges that Patuxent has received

a flood of politicized and radical prisoners, mostly black, who weren't going to be broken and weren't going to suck up to white middle-class orthodox "psychiatry" in order to wheedle their way out, all of which took Patuxent's administration very much by surprise. (pp. 110–11)

Boslow *et al.* [18] report that at Patuxent

those inmates who remain residents of the first or lowest tier level are *characteristically younger in age,* have somewhat lower IQ, *are often Negroes,* and typically come from homes that were broken or disorganized from infancy on, and that had a malignant psychological climate. (p. 5, emphasis added)

If we make provision for predictable discrepancies in a language, both statements point to a culture gap between purveyors and refusers of treatment.

This fact makes it reprehensible to insist on retaining the refusers in treatment programs instead of reintegrating them into the general prison population. To define an inmate as a treatment candidate even if he persistently refuses treatment provides integrity to accusations of calculated mistreatment, and serves ho useful purpose. But it does more than that: it engages treaters in unseemly and degrading interactions that involve the use of force. The net result of such conflicts is to demonstrate the impotence of treaters who seek to impose treatment on those bent on resisting it at all costs.

The Legitimacy of Therapy

The obduracy of inmate resistances to treatment hinges partly on our failure to convince inmates that we have selected them fairly and that we are intervening minimally and appropriately. If men feel equitably sentenced and are classified in terms of their conduct, the questions that arise are fewer than if incarceration and diagnosis seem arbitrary. Patuxent patients are a case in point, because they can easily see their adjudication as capricious. Commitment to Patuxent involves a criminal conviction, but subsequent to this juncture, any prosecutor or prison warden may ask for a defective delinquency hearing, which tests the assumption that the man may be more dangerous than his crime and presentence assessment indicate. This option must be seen as double jeopardy, even if it is applied to every demonstrably violent offender and to no one else. But in Maryland a man need have done nothing violent to be scrutinized and warehoused for "dangerousness." Though the situation has changed, in 1958 the bulk of the Patuxent inmates were burglars and thiefs. The list of other conviction offenses included abortion, conspiracy, desertion, disorderly conduct, embezzlement, escape, false pretenses, forgery, motor vehicle larceny, distribution of obscene literature, roguery, soliciting, uttering, and violation of probation of parole [148, pp. 12-14].

The next step in the process (the adjudication of defective delinquency) involves a new trial, which centers on the recommendation of a psychiatric panel, and follows this recommendation over 80 percent of the time. Strangely enough, the psychiatric panel consists of Patuxent staff, which means that the judge or jury can commit an inmate to the care of men who have labeled him risky, who have called him "defective" and who have lengthened his term to a possible life sentence.[a]

Maryland legislators, Patuxent, and the courts concur in assuming that a

[a]Ironically, Patuxent staff imply that it is the jury's decision, rather than the psychiatric panel's recommendation, which may be unfair. Boslow and Kohlmeyer [20] write that "we have found on a statistical basis that juries are most likely to release young offenders who are somewhat angelic in appearance and who meet all the stereotyped requirements for being the All American Boy. It is especially effective if the patient's mother is there to weep for him on the witness stand" (p. 121).

type of dangerous person exists who is described in the "defective delinquency" law under which the men are committed. The heading covers men who, "by the demonstration of persistent aggravated antisocial or criminal behavior, evidence a propensity toward criminal activity and who (are) found to have either such intellectual deficiency or emotional unbalance, or both, so as to clearly demonstrate an actual danger to society" [40, Section 5].

The psychiatrists are presumed capable of determining whether a man has an "intellectual deficiency or emotional unbalance" that makes him dangerous. If psychiatrists make this diagnosis, the inmate is invited to concede they might be right. All of this is supposed to occur despite the fact that the key phraseology is very unflattering to the inmate.

Patuxent staff know that "emotional unbalance" is not a precise term. Boslow, Rosenthal, and Gliedman [22] write that

Since no individual can be reasonably said to have achieved perfect emotional balance, whatever that may mean, we could presumably infer that every individual showed some degree of emotional unbalance. Thus, with this kind of interpretation of the term, which is akin to sophistry, we could commit as a defective delinquent any individual who engaged in persistent anti-social behavior which constituted a danger to society. (p. 6)

In order to limit the range of emotional unbalance to a meaningful syndrome, we are told that "case history criteria and clinical impressions" are used to locate the type of man

who has not been truly socialized and who recognizes no true loyalties. He is basically amoral, shares minimal social values with others, and is flagrantly hedonistic and opportunistic. His crimes are of impulse, sometimes of a compulsive, neurotic nature, and usually involve inadequate planning at best. (p. 7)

We are told that such a person is "someone who is at the mercy of his needs or impulses" or suffers from "the lack of organized controls of behavior we call ego-strength" (p. 8).

It is hard to see how any offender could grant the validity of a label that is documented by the "clinical" impression that his own ego is "poorly" developed, and that he responds overreadily to his needs. Worse, one wonders whether "hedonistic" and "opportunistic" mean that a man could be deemed "defective" for being obnoxious (see chapter 6) or for having grown up in a part of town in which the ego attributes prized by Patuxent staff would look silly. We have pointed out elsewhere that the conventional "mature ego" may prove useless in environments such as the urban ghetto, where structural resources are scarce. In such environments, well-functioning egos may have attributes different from those described in the traditional psychoanalytic literature. For example,

In a human jungle, the ego that sells immediacy short would be pounced upon and consumed. In a world of dead ends, the person who hopes and plans would be pounding his head against predictable walls. . . .

In a situation in which opportunities are blocked, the ego should become a mechanism designed to make hay in the few moments the sun is shining. It should feast and famine and must oscillate between ecstasy and resignation. It should play for luck and develop a respect for fate and its import. Such an ego, needless to say, would meet with contempt for its hedonism, its low time perspective, its passivity. It would invite efforts at therapy and reformation [177, p. 390].

The situation is not helped by the fact that the courts have held that designations such as "psychopath" and "sociopath" are vague, and if they were used to classify violence-prone inmates, would make the process unconstitutional [38, pp. 6 ff.]. Although Patuxent officially avoids flagrant labelling, it issues research publications that refer to inmate-subjects as "sociopathic criminals" or "severely sociopathic" [80, 81, 187]. On the opposite extreme, Patuxent staff argue that their inmates are a hopelessly confused melange, which requires sorting into meaningful groups. Boslow et al. [18] tell us that "our inmate population is a very heterogeneous one. One of our goals is to be able to define this population in terms of various sub-types" (p. 13). It is hard to conceive of a patient with access to Patuxent literature who could make sense of the fact that he is described as a "severe sociopath" on the one hand, and as an unknown quantity on the other. It might also disturb the patient to read that the "risk" the psychiatrists take in classifying him "is not tempered by a wide background of experience or by a generally accepted set of criteria which have been tested and upheld," and that "experience and criteria can come only with time and much careful research" [18, pp. 10-11].

After the inmate has raised questions about his arrival at Patuxent, he may ponder the issue of his release. But the view here is no brighter, because in order to be discharged a man must convince those who classed him as "defective" that he has become "nondefective." Since psychiatrists are unlikely to admit error, the man must show that he has become discriminably different. Here he is not helped by the fact that clinical criteria such as "impulsivity," "weak ego," and "emotional unbalance" are hard to translate into behavior. How would an inmate go about making himself less impulsive, or improving the quality of his ego? It seems almost impossible for a man faced with such a task not to try to diagnose the assumptions and predilections of his judges, and to play these inferences back in some fashion.

Such a game becomes more complex if one considers a third fact. Classifiers and releasers are also the treaters. In other words, the Patuxent staff who have seen the inmate as "defective," and who must change their minds, must also see themselves as responsible for the man's transformation. This means that the inmate needs to know (1) what makes him look "defective" to psychiatrists,

(2) what impression he must provide to appear "nondefective," and (3) how he can appear responsive to the staff's treatment efforts.

The Reward Structure

Given this challenge—and the compromise of self that is required—why would anyone try? Patuxent's answer is "incentives." In addition to the desire for freedom, there is the controlled quality of prison life. Inmates who "progress" can earn tangible advances in their standard of living. Patuxent has four vertically arranged tiers, each of which improves upon the environment of the tiers below it. This arrangement permits staff to dispense immediate and foreseeable rewards to its clients.

Any prison uses its living environment to reward and punish. Segregation is a substandard milieu usually invoked to discourage serious misconduct. To start a *reward* sequence at a substandard level would be clearly confusing. It would imply punishment without cause, and could constitute a violation of a person's right not to be penalized beyond the decision of courts. Patuxent's first stage has thus been condemned by Mitford as a place where one is "deliberately subjected to the unalloyed punishment of solitary lock-up, held virtually incommunicado in a nine-by-six-foot cell for almost twenty-four hours a day, denied books, letters, visitors, allowed but one shower a week" [92, pp. 109-10]. A Patuxent staff member disagrees. He notes that "the (first tier) facilities probably compare favorably with any other institution's facilities in (Maryland). The cells are as spacious and meet American Correctional Association standards, all have plumbing and electrical facilities, are single occupancy, and have privileges and facilities that meet or exceed those in other general population units" [26].

Whatever the actual situation, "higher" tiers at Patuxent (like most "hospital" environments) are clearly more comfortable than the average prison. According to Meister [87], inmates feel that Patuxent

brings them into sustained contact with persons other than inmates and guards, persons who treat them systematically with a degree of respect unheard of elsewhere, inside *or* outside prison. They are taken seriously, they think, and they like that. (p. 38)

In other prisons, environmental manipulation is usually used without assuming that it is "treatment." San Quentin, for instance, has a social structure that an inmate (Fioritto) recently described as follows:

All of the inmates living in San Quentin are no doubt aware of the "class" structure of San Quentin. A new man arrives and ordinarily starts out on the bottom rung of the ladder which is known as A section. He then is classified by the institution and customarily assigned work duties. Unless he is assigned to culinary duties, his next move is usually to the east block. The population there consists of a hodgepodge of individuals, some unassigned. This level is pretty much limited as to extra-curricular activities and extra privileges.

After the man has a certain amount of "clean time," i.e., time with no disciplinary actions, his next step is to move to the north block. There, the men enjoy a little more freedom. They are allowed to participate in night activities such as college and are considered by staff to be less of a violence risk.

In approximately 18 months after arrival here, a man becomes eligible for the honor unit which is the west block. After 18 months of good conduct, staff feels that a man is capable of handling a less restrictive situation. West block is the highest level an inmate can achieve within this institution.

Along with its many other privileges, west block has their own exercise yard [153].

Patuxent, unlike San Quentin, would defend its social structure as treatment rather than as reward for compliance. The distinction lies in the contention that staff is not rewarding behavior that makes for a more congenial institution and less trouble for staff, but behavior that (1) marks an improvement in the inmate's way of relating to others, and (2) transfers to real life so as to produce a nonviolence-prone citizen.

There are two difficulites here: One is the fact that congenial inmates generally tend to be viewed as making progress. Although clinical progress may be signalled by panic, acting out or turmoil (a fact characterized by Redl [142] as "the improvement mess"), it is hard to conceive of an inmate being rewarded for "healthy" conduct if he disrupts the life of staff. This makes it difficult to prove that "maturity" or "mental health" are every really judged.[b] The second problem lies in evidence that suggests that rewarded progress in institutions tends to decay in noninstitutional settings.

Token economy programs, which use institutional rewards systematically, have converted backward schizophrenics from vegetables to functioning human beings; they have taught dropouts to read; they have made disruptive youths in institutions responsible and cooperative as lambs. But such gains have tended to be lost in "real life" social structures with "real life" reward systems. The patients regress, the youths recidivate, and the violence prone renew their destructive careers. Community adjustment is only achieved where the patient

---

[b]The difficulty of disentangling criteria cuts various ways at Patuxent. Boslow and Kohlmeyer [20] point out that "The (Patuxent) Classification Committee ... considers *cooperativeness and attitudes of the patients,* and may ... demote them within the tier system for *lack of interest* in the rehabilitative efforts" (p. 132, emphasis added); the same writers note that "the sentencing by (the Patuxent Disciplinary) Committee is utilized *as a tool to influence behavior* of the offenders rather than to punish them" [20, p. 122, emphasis added]. In other words, rewards are tied to the patient's willingness to cooperate, and punishments are incentives to good conduct. Both criteria are more arbitrary than those of custodial settings, where advancement follows productivity, and punishment responds to infractions.

or inmate is provided with "bridging" experiences that help him evolve coping skills under conditions of increased freedom [6, 46].

A Bridge to Reality

Patuxent in actual fact furnishes five graded tiers, with the fifth (parole) probably having the most "treatment" potential. The level consists of work release, and regular weekly involvement in the Patuxent Out-Patient Clinic:

This Clinic is an extension of the Institution in that it is staffed by those psychiatrists, psychologists, and social workers with whom the patient has been in close contact during his stay at Patuxent. Psychotherapy, both group and individual, is continued in a consistent manner with personnel with whom the patient is familiar. He no longer feels alone in a hostile world in which he has to bare his soul to strangers. Rapport has been built up over a period of time with people who are perceived as accepting, trusted, and interested [79, p. 2].

Patuxent's "fifth tier" combines two virtues that we find in other successful "semisheltered" or "halfway house" settings: (1) the client can rehearse his skills and reactions in nonartificial situations, which permits him (and us) to sensibly assess his strengths and weaknesses; and (2) in the absence of outside props (constraints and rewards), a man finds out whether he really wants help.

A third advantage is the fact that outside prison a man can accept treatment without compromising his integrity. He can react to staff, and not to staff power; he need not fear peers; he can afford honesty and openness.

In closed settings, men play games. We never know when, how much, and how they are playing them. Where some men pretend, others comply; there are also those who grow. In all cases, we overestimate the impact of staff power. Inmates can—and do—fool us. Although there are men who superficially conform or resist, others undergo tangible and substantial change. We see neither fact. Some of us (treaters) assume congenial clients; others (critics) assume stern resistance. We forget that inmates have needs beyond those they like to talk about—needs that are not easily seen nor simplistically conceptualized. We forget that men in prison know failure. They have reason to suspect that their conduct has spelled trouble, and that it might do so again.

It is more important that change clients be ready, than that they be willing.[c] Men who demand treatment may wish nurturance. They may want support and props. They may enlist help so as to remain helpless, passive, child-like, and ineffectual [172]. Other men may fight intervention tooth and nail, but in

---

[c]Freud [49] felt that skepticism in a patient was no bar to effective therapy. He tells us that "this attitude on the part of the patient has very little importance; his preliminary belief or disbelief is almost negligible compared with the inner resistances which hold the neurosis fast" (p. 138).

the course of battle may gain insight. Stormy treatment may have a good chance of success [47].

A whole slew of problems arise when we ask whether an inmate's participation in a program is, or can be, "voluntary." A man who is compulsively driven, obsessively bent, characterized by loss of self-control or reinforced by dependency needs is not autonomous when he "does his thing." It is not obvious that when such a person "exercises his right not to be subjected to treatment" (if treatment is an intervention designed to free him from internal restraints) he is in the same boat with the man who refuses to be indoctrinated. We may at least demand an honest effort to recruit the nonarbitrarily assigned client, who needs therapy and who can benefit from the type of therapy we have available, and to share with him the logic of our diagnosis and the prospects and dangers we see for him. We can then create a situation where the man can really participate in his own regeneration if he wants to [176].

A variant on this notion is Norval Morris' suggestion that the special treatment candidate be provided with time in which to "case" a program before committing himself to it. Morris proposes that

the selected prisoners should come to the institution . . . to find out what the institution is really like—long enough to see beyond the physical surroundings to the hard work and discipline of serious introspection and the prospect of facing one's own problems. During this time the exact nature of the institution would be set out by, in effect, negotiating an individualized contract with each prisoner based on his past, his present situation, and his anamnestic prognosis [93, p. 96].

This procedure might have benefits for staff. It is compatible with the suggestion of Freud [49] that a "provisional" or "trial" therapy of two weeks be employed "to learn more about the case and to decide whether it is a suitable one for psychoanalysis" (p. 136).

Therapeutic Communities

In a variety of institutional programs, men have been made partners in their regeneration. Token economies are often run with clients involved in determining the "scales" of rewarded conduct, or in dispensing tokens [6]. In prisons, inmates have met with guards to resolve questions of ethics and to fix standards of discipline [154].

The principle of client participation has been annunciated in the classic model of the "therapeutic community," originated by Maxwell Jones [66]. This model entails a partnership between treaters and clients, and a blurring of the traditional roles of "patient" and "therapist."

The paradigm—as developed with shell-shocked troops during World War II—

involves the creation of an intimate, staff–client social world in the institutional setting. Attention focuses on the reactions of community members toward each other, and on the way each person's conduct is perceived by others. Every interpersonal event becomes a "living-learning" opportunity for everyone in the group.

Community meetings provide the opportunity for the discussion and analysis of personal encounters. Democratic organization, including inmate self-government and interchangeable staff roles make for more flexible games than those premised on staff expertise and power. Community problems mirror real-life problems, permitting individual pathology to surface instead of stimulating stereotyped institutional reactions.

This model has been used in Scandinavia in an institution designed for the "untreatable" offender [168]. A more radical application to violent offenders is that of Barker and his colleagues in Penetanguishene, Ontario. Penetanguishene is a psychiatric institution in which clients do therapy, and where they participate in clinical decisions about each other. Barker tells us that "the patient is in many ways better equipped than the professional for a direct, helpful encounter" [10, p. 63]. The patient is always there; he has no formal role to protect; his suffering and his desire to get well create strong bonds with others. Having personal problems is an impediment, but according to Barker and Mason [10],

pathologies cancel and reciprocate one another. To give a very crude example, a schizophrenic will object to the slick solution to a problem adeptly flashed out by a psychopath. The psychopath will point with some justice to the wooliness and diffuse idealism of the schizophrenic. Or again, no one can so unerringly highlight the subtle manipulations of a severely sick psychopath as one who is similarly crazy. No one can perceive the first crumblings of a schizophrenic disintegration more quickly than one who has once similarly collapsed himself. (p. 63).

Barker's faith in the "sanity" of violent men is reflected in the administrative structure of his ward. Patient committees on steering, welfare, medication, and small groups/crisis administer the program; patients make parole recommendations; clinical matters are in the hands of a group on assesssment. An executive group (four patients and two staff members) deals with policy issues.

Innovative treatment at Penetanguishene is often patient designed. For instance, safety problems created by destructive or self-destructive explosions of patients became of concern to "a schizophrenic who had murdered three persons" and led him to propose a brilliant therapeutic modality. The patient argued

that the best way he could see of protecting someone from his own anxiety was to have someone else with him all the time. He suggested to his skeptical peers at a ward meeting that this could be simply achieved by joining them with a locked strap at the wrist. . . . Patients designed a strap about 18 inches long made of car seatbelt material . . . this strap becomes a durable handcuff. . . . By a simple arrangement of patients and shifts, each potentially homicidal or suicidal patient is constantly in the presence of another patient who is better integrated and responsible for seeing that he does not harm himself or anyone else [11, pp. 2–3].

This particular innovation was one that had a combination of benefits; it permitted anxious patients to continue functioning as full-fledged community members; it gave them feedback when they expressed anxiety, and it showed them the concern of their fellows. The procedure gave patient-crisis managers the chance to play a complex and constructive role. This feature is important in the therapeutic community, where patients experience the impact of role shifts. The patient in Penetanguishene thus learns about being "worker, committee member, helper and patient":

in some settings, he was treated. In some, he was the treater. Often, he might occupy both roles simultaneously. . . . The individual was forced to pull himself together, sanely, to help someone else [10, p. 68].

Penetanguishene knows that peer-run programs can spawn exploitive games. The institution's staff seeks to neutralize this danger by (1) systematic groupings of weak and strong inmates, and by (2) the "here-and-now" emphasis of patient interactions. This emphasis matters, because it prevents men from gaining power over others by playing a formal "therapist" role [9, p. 2].

But groups of inmates in such a system do exercise a great deal of power. The new patient learns that

where he went and what he did, from seven in the morning until ten at night, seven days a week, was determined by his fellow patients in a committee. The small group treatment he received, the medication he took, the penalties of his deviance were all fixed by the appropriate patient groups. He might be called upon by a committee to observe through the night in the Intensive Care Unit, be handcuffed to a dangerous patient, assist in carrying a man bodily to treatment, search a man for razor blades, or a room for broken glass. He might be deprived of his room, his clothes, his mattress, his coffee, or his tobacco, by a committee. As a last resort, he might be stripped by them, and locked in a screened room [10, p. 69].

This influence is characterized by Barker and Mason as "at an extreme remove from the gangsterism of a reform institution inmate subculture" (p. 69). There is reciprocity because the patients—unlike prison inmates—can freely shape their culture. There is concern among them for the welfare of others and the climate of their ward.

Not all features of Penetanguishene seem constructive, nor are they all congruent with a therapeutic community emphasis. There are faddish interventions (nude encounter) and risky ones (hallucinogenes). But the distinguishing feature of this program and of other self-therapizing communities seems revolutionary and fresh. It enables us to conceive of institutional environments in which inmate-staff games and peer exploitation are not automatic by-products of imprisonment.

Staff Roles

In conventional prisons, treatment can be drowned out or coopted. Treaters can become ugly ducklings, cinderellas, window dressing, or concessions to liberalism. Psychiatrists may be used strictly as crisis managers for problem cases or soothsayers of risk. In "mainline" decisions, such as those of classification and management, custodial personnel may decide mental health matters (e.g., how to handle potential victims or exploiters), and invoke custodial criteria for their decisions. On occasions, an officer may admit that mental health knowledge (diagnostic pointers or hints on management) might be germane, but such an officer would be an exception.

Although custody is viewed as the main function of prisons, it loses its glamour in "treatment"-oriented settings, and may be labeled a necessary, distasteful service. Custodial recommendations may be overridden by "therapeutic" considerations, and officers may (correctly) see themselves degraded or disrespected. Meister [87] talked with Patuxent guards who

tell us that of all the visitors to their model institution we are the first to visit them. . . . In the name of therapy, the guards claim, the administration coddles the inmates; the inmates con the therapists; and both are in league against the guards, who consider the ideology and practice of therapy at Patuxent a dangerous "con game," with rules and language which effectively exclude them. (p. 37)

At Patuxent the talk among staff and inmates revolves heavily around mental health concerns. Guards are subjected to compulsory psychology lectures and are stereotyped as antitherapeutic. Professional staff feel they have "discovered" that "the attitudes reflected by our officers seemed to be in opposition to the work of therapists" [19, p. 27]. The approach of psychiatrists to their "discovery" has been a barrage of one-way communication, and a circumscription of the officers' power. Although guards are nominally members of treatment teams, their role is clearly ancillary. Patuxent has assumed that "to teach security personnel to be behavioral scientists requires additional college or graduate level training and considerable time" [19, p. 31]. The assumption here is that treatment is the purview of mental health professionals.

Correctional officers are locked into custodial definitions of their roles as a result of psychiatric definitions of the therapeutic role. But Jones [66] and others have shown us that there are different models, which can define treatment more generously, and can accommodate staff more broadly as members of intervention "teams."

The custodial officer, like the inmate, is a resource of considerable power. Officers have opportunities to observe their charges in diverse situations, and can interact with them in natural, nonartificial ways. Officers can gather information about inmate difficulites; they can run groups; they can work as team members, with inmate-aides, counselors, chaplains, psychiatrists. To do these things they must be defined (and must define themselves) as human service agents.

The Why and Wherefore of Treatment

In chapter 6 we suggested that the most obvious way of selecting treatment candidates is to pick people with social or personal deficits—particularly people who would profit from the interventions we have available. We suggested that other criteria must apply where we select people for different purposes, such as men who have been dangerous, and are presumed risks. We know that a man who has been violent must be treated with circumspection, but we do not know that such a man is a candidate for guided group interaction or a prospective member for a token economy.

Keeping our decisions separate makes logical sense. More crucial, it is a practical necessity. In Patuxent, for example, the combined sentencing-treatment-release process places patients and staff into impossible situations and creates awkward relationships. The inmate resists treatment because he feels himself unreasonably selected for treatment candidacy; he pretends to comply so as to be released from the bonds of indeterminacy. Even where he is appropriately treated, he can see himself unjustly incarcerated or unreasonably held.

It is nice if treaters have time, but it is not necessary. Long sentences may help. But a short sentence is a challenge for treaters to do the best they can in the time they have. It may even enhance their work. Freud recommends fixing terminal dates for complacent patients, and he notes that this often inspires serious efforts to change [48].

Risk is the business of parole boards. Some men are poor risks after lifetimes of therapy; for others, time heals. If program participation is considered by parole boards in assessing risk, inmates must know this and consider the fact in deciding how to do their time. But we must not insist on treatment as the key to freedom, for it has goals that have integrity of their own.

Treatment can be generously viewed. Equating it with formal therapy (as we often do) is a luxury. It restricts help to a select few. It abandons the many. It creates Patuxents that "treat," and custodial warehouses that do not. Both custodial and psychiatric prisons are prisons. Their climates are violence prone. They feature defensive subcultures, and defensive interactions between and among inmates and staff.

Settings exemplified by the therapeutic milieu model aim at different types of climates. They seek high participation, and loose roles. And they treat. For in such settings, "living" means "learning," and "learning" means "treatment." Resources deployed elsewhere in existing or surviving (among inmates) or in managing and protecting (among staff) become treatment resources. All men must teach and all men must learn. Even a violent man can make an impact on other men if he learns to be accepted by them without resorting to violence as the tool.

8 Peacekeeping

Arrest is unwelcome and jail confining. Prisons harbor hardened and violent men. Yet, few officers and suspects are killed, few guards are injured, few inmates maimed.

Violence is harnessed in police and prison settings, as elsewhere. Men are "socialized" and they solve most of their problems nonviolently, through talk or through action. Most men have learned to do so, and, to a lesser extent, they are constrained to do so. In private contacts, violence can bring retaliation or disdain. In organizations, there are rules. Violence risks security loss or invites punishment.

Nonetheless we do have "violence problems." We have them where men feel they *must* use violence, or where they *do not care whether they are violent.* They act in defiance of rules where they feel driven to it, or where they take the rules lightly. In doing so, they obey rules and norms of their own. Their violence reflects violence-prone socialization, group pressures, norms, threats, incentives.

The balance of the norms to which a man hearkens—of the "driving" and "restraining" forces to violence—shifts constantly. In today's prisons, and in police confrontations, it is shifting toward a higher regard for violence. New tensions, tougher men, tighter groups and increased alienation help. Violence brings fear, challenge, hate, and new violence. With escalation, reforms become harder to achieve but also more urgent to address. New variables must be understood, harnessed, and countered, and new change options must be exercised.

Self-esteem and Violence

We have been stressing the importance of "machismo" in police and prison contexts. We have suggested that we expect violence where men rely on combative indices of self-worth, such as toughness and bravery. We have argued that among criminal justice clients, machismo translates into exploitation of one's peers and defiance of staff. We have also seen how staff can become oversensitive to client challenges and can become obsessed with the need to control clients.

Macho norms arise where other sources of esteem are scarce. And such norms can be unwittingly reinforced by the emphasis of social systems, such as the criminal justice system: Organizations can foster machismo where they include or stress combativeness among official or among informal roads to recognition, status or advancement.

109

Predominantly male organizations need not intrinsically prize physical conduct norms. Monasteries emphasize spiritually, corporate boards reward business acumen, and academic communities have (at times) sought wisdom. Such enterprises may be largely or exclusively male, without accents on physical prowess and bravery.

But in other settings, working-class male values are adopted and accentuated, and pressures accumulate for displays of manliness. Such pressures permeate even ostensible human service agencies, such as probation offices where staff sport weapons.

In the police case, machismo is part of the "prestige arrest" syndrome. While the reward system does not center on physical destruction, it highlights valor and daring. Citations for humane acts, for interpersonal acumen or for good community relations may be accorded, but rarely. For prison guards, the problem is more a lack of any type of rewards. There are few roles as inhospitable as the custodial one. Although a policeman must often cope with boredom, his work is exciting compared with that of custody, with its endless routine of escorting and counting. The dilemma of correctional clients is most obvious. Suspects in police encounters face their own powerlessness; so do custody or therapy inmates. They must compensate wherever they can; physical indexes are the traditional means of demonstrating one's worth as a man.

For both staff and clients, peer groups fill voids of status. Toughness, coolness, the need to "instill respect," readiness to meet aggression, self-insulation, become shared measures of the "good" cop, inmate, suspect or guard. Even "good" therapists can be admired for inviolability and stoicism.

Such group norms intersect to form climates, which may be stable, as with a "respected" police force or a "cool" prison. Here, men go about their collective business, maintaining separateness or distance, and infringing minimally on others. Tension occurs where compensatory coping offends victims or opponents, and where the use of others to gain self-esteem escalates through retaliation or contagion.

Subcultural Norms and Violence

In thinking of group pressures and violence, the relationship most familiar to us is that of the "subculture of violence" [196]. We think of groups that encourage or legitimize violent responses to stimuli that nonmembers of such groups would react to nonviolently. Violence subcultures can exist among an agency's staff in the shape of "goon squads," and they can exist among clients in more or less formalized gangs.

But the context of most of the violence we have been discussing is different. It takes the shape of the Many disregarding and protecting violence by the Few. It represents cynicism about the world that prizes a retreatist or hands-off stance at the expense of promoting peace and serving the common good.

Subcultures of this kind reflect alienation or an absence of community. They reflect the ethnocentric or egocentric orientation of men who sense no rewards, and suspect danger, in departing from parochial goals. The loyalty of such men is to their own kind, no matter how individually reprehensible they are, because the larger setting is seen as impersonal and threatening. Such men feel they have no stake in the larger community, and they see themselves as having much to lose and little to gain by trying to relate to the world at large.

There is conflict, as men see it, of endangered interests. Clients and staff are "at war," because each *feels* at war with the other. Only the weak and vulnerable feel otherwise, and become rats, informers, pawns.

Alienation is a breeding ground for escalation. While violent men are not admired by their peers, they are seen as behaving understandably. Their conduct is accepted and condoned, because reality is seen as war and war is seen as violent.

Like the fruit fly, the organizational norm is not born full blown. Alienated men in criminal justice settings inherit their norms partly from alienated and defensive groups that exist in the community. Street gangs enter the prison yard, and young cynical working-class men hang their coats in staff locker rooms.

But importing divisive norms does not predestine them to permanence. Organizations are small and tight enough to evolve community in ways that street corners cannot evolve it. But to achieve such community entails the evolution of accepted means and shared goals. This requires that we first diagnose violence-promoting norms, then establish goals and rules, identify means, and, ultimately, make goals and means shareable.

Means and Ends

Deemphasizing the behavior rules of the criminal justice game can bring violence through carelessness. Such is the case with airline pilots who discuss baseball scores while landing instead of reviewing altitude readings, and it holds for police officers who casually approach men with guns.

Ritualization is equally dangerous. Where means are ends, inflexibility brings danger. Static situations are escalated through "routine precautions," while real threats are ignored by canned approaches. An officer who meets traffic stops with gun drawn is as violence prone as one who ignores panic in stolen-car drivers. The guard who "never talks to a con" is as vulnerable as one who curries universal love.

An "anything goes" view of means has a way of including violence. The "wise guy" on the beat or the opposing hockey player in a cut-throat game may be casually dealt with because "it doesn't really matter." A similar stance can justify the rape of inmates, and undergirds poetry in report writing.

On the other hand, overemphasizing means for their own sake makes power a goal. It relegates "why" or "what for" issues to quibbles. It demands conforming inmates, "good patients," and passive suspects, with no concern for subsurface problems, such as lingering grievances or the paucity of over-due change. A psychiatric ward with pliable, lethargic patients is a testimonial to bankruptcy. The zombies of today have no incentive for not becoming the zombies of tomorrow. Violent men have no reason not to remain violence prone.

Professionalization, in the best sense of the word, implies that means matter, and that they relate to ends. Skill means little if it is not understood and consciously used as the way of achieving goals effectively and humanely. Problem solving includes a concern for ethics and pragmatics. With diminished regard for consequence or proportionality, force—however effectively applied—is always violence. The surgeon who exquisitely but unnecessarily operates is a butcher. Although skilled, he is nonprofessional The same holds for an armed-to-the-teeth police force, trained in karate and the use of sophisticated weaponry. Such an organization is less "professional" than a ragamuffin conglomerate of paunchy, ill-equipped nonathletes who exercise ingenuity in resolving explosive situations as nonviolently as they can.

Compromise Goals

We have suggested that one reason why violence is obdurate is because organizational missions include latent or unspoken themes that encourage it. In sports, for instance, a competitive stance, buttressed by "go gettum" lineup talks and taunts from the stands creates a climate antithetical to gentlemanliness. Pressures arise from enforcement goals in police agencies and custody goals in prisons which make physical control of clients (and resistance by clients) equally tempting concerns.

Fortunately, police and prisons do not exist at peace with their goals. For police, the "crime-fighting" goal is nominally dominant, but it describes rare acts and rarer rewards. It leaves much police work undefined, and the rest is called "enforcement" on tenuous or ambiguous grounds.

Such semantics have consequences when the officer faces a belligerent drunk, an angry husband, or an unruly crowd. Behavioral options are restricted when stimulus situations are viewed primarily in "enforcement" terms.

Police seek resources to lower crime rates, implying that police services reduce crime. Should the crime impact of police be undemonstrated, the syllogism can backfire. Hard-strapped communities can curtail their police departments. And while police retrenchment may not encourage crime, it can reduce the quality of citizen life. This can happen because police are our unadvertised nonspecialized front line service agency, providing emergency assistance to the sick, to the emotionally disturbed, and to victims of accidents and mishaps.

The crime-fighting police myth produces "numbers games" played with acts such as traffic tickets, which reduces the use of nonenforcement options (such as warnings or counseling) that often make a great deal more sense. On the other end of the spectrum, police can abandon or overlook some crucial community problems (such as consumer fraud) because the heavy emphasis on street crime makes it inviting to define such areas as "civil" matters. As a result, officers who could be cultivating grateful clients spend their time in adversary encounters with minor offenders.

Despite much talk of "rehabilitation," prisons tend to be little more than warehouses. The problem is not the rigidity of prison goals, but goals that are arrived at by default. Custody is what prisons do while they wait for something better to come along. It is the nonreducable minimum that is required of an institution which receives clients and must retain them safely until they are released. It is a holding pattern in the absence of landing instructions. Custody is neither a lofty goal for staff, nor an appealing one for clients. It is not the subject prison managers address in speeches. It is not a way to reduce crime. It provides nothing to show for itself. Neither inmates nor staff have anything to gain from custodial goals.

Rehabilitation skeptics talk of "humane warehousing" as prison's goal. The term is at minimum a paradox. Humaneness implies a responsiveness to client needs, which requires rendering noncustodial services. It is not "humane" to mount guard on an inmate-in-panic, and to let him stew. No "humanitarian" notifies a man of his mother's death, and proceeds to remove his shoe laces and belt. "Humaneness" means watching for feelings, and addressing them through classification, counselling, and other helping or regenerating services. It also means attending to the social environment, to provide for the need of the prisoner for stability, privacy and quiet. To define "humaneness" under "custody" distorts such services, makes them invisible, highlights mechanical staff functions, and sweeps staff–inmate links under a semantic rug.

Inmates as custody clients tend to feel rejected as human service clients. Their standard adjustment to the custodial role (trying to neutralize staff) creates a survival perspective that minimizes the chance of inmates caring for each other. In the face of all the vulnerabilities and despair that emerge through institutionalization, the premium remains on each inmate doing his time, or— worse—on inmates building their self-esteem at the expense of each others' misery.

New Goals and Functions

Police and prisons clearly live with unmet needs among citizens and clients that are not provided for in current definitions of organizational missions. With police, the fault has rested in the highlighting of goals that were (wrongly) considered prestigious. Prisons have too often been content to take bare minimum custody duties seriously as a definition of mission.

Inventories of *needs* help to identify *goals.* Police and prisons can, by attending to staff and client problems that are currently being ignored, arrive at statements of organizational goals that make more sense and cause less strain than current conceptions of agency mission.

Police

Police interface with more service needs than any other agency. Officers work at strange hours and in strange places, while most other human service agents are restricted by nine-to-five schedules, and by lack of outreach. Unlike other agencies, police have more power and access: they can invoke law; they can criminalize, decriminalize, arrest, commit, refer.

What police agencies are not doing is facing their involvements—the full gamut of their involvements—with pride. Police departments fail to recognize all that police officers do, and do exclusively, necessarily, and well. The organizational reluctance to face service involvements is easily explained. To face a service role means thinking of police as preserving the peace, not as "combatting" crime. It also means dropping the illusion that police are always champions of law, whose hand is forced by breaches of law. It entails police recognizing that they exercise wide discretion, and that this discretion may be deployed to solve complex human problems.

The challenge is one of explicitly expanding and developing police functions that are not combative, but that respond to gaps in municipal services. It means joining hands with nonconflict-oriented agencies in service delivery arrangements (teams, referral networks) that permit effective response to breaches of peace and victimization.

The core role of policing makes such a coordinating role appropriate. Police take up slack of citizen protection (municipal "police" power) where more restricted and specialized agencies leave vacuums; unlike *every* other service agency, police have the broadest of mandates. They can invoke laws, and can decide whether the victimization of any citizen is serious enough to represent a public (rather than civil or private) affront. The more generously the police draw this line, the more likely they are to earn the gratitude and esteem of the weak, who are the most alienated from government.

Prisons

Whatever else prisons are, they are wasteful. They contain thousands of persons —staff and inmates—who are minimally involved in meaningful effort. Inmates make license plates and play checkers. Staff watch inmates. In watching inmates, staff "protect" the rest of us. While inmates play checkers, they are not robbing banks or mugging people. If inmates play checkers long enough, they become too old to rob banks. Even better, they may learn to hate prison so much that they will refrain from mugging and robbing people so as not to return to prison.

The investment is too large for the result. Two few inmates are in prison for too short a time to protect us. Released inmates show too little trace of having been deterred. Gauging prisons in terms of crime reduction shows them wanting as well as wasteful.

Prison as a measure is too strong, the suffering it occasions too obvious, and the waste it entails too real to let matters rest. But since men will continue to be sent to prison, we cannot fool ourselves (as many experts do) with pleas for decarceration. Where "diversion" from prison occurs, there is no millenium. We know that (1) community resources have mandates just as ambiguous as prisons; (2) "graduates" of community treatment often are prison inmates later; and (3) diversion makes prisons the repositories of more serious offenders and may increase their custodial thrust.

The last point is critical. It suggests that where in the past prisons have been merely wasteful and ineffective, they are now wasteful, ineffective, and in trouble. Increased violence levels are an index of a degenerating condition—most serious (as in California) where decarceration is most widely used.

In any crisis, there are incentives and motives for change. Some innovations we have reviewed—grievance reforms, therapeutic community experiments, etc.—suggest new flexibility in corrections. We may now be ready for a really serious inventory of—and attack on—correctional problems or "needs."

Examples of such problems are the needs for developing better means of (1) assisting more vulnerable inmates, who have difficulty surviving in prison, (2) grouping and assigning compatible staff and inmates, (3) using staff to provide services and mental health assistance acceptable to clients, (4) resolving interpersonal and group conflicts and tension, (5) sustaining and stabilizing relationships between inmates and their significant others in the community, and (6) diagnosing personal and social deficits of inmates, and addressing these deficits through treatment. These examples (and others like them) are paths along which prisons can develop and implement new human service goals. And since the product of prison is the reintegrated ex-inmate, the prison must take an open-system approach to at least some of its goals. Ideally, it can evolve programs in which staff and inmates can serve the community as they help themselves.

Expanding Human Services

Expanding human services in the criminal justice system can reduce violence because it (1) builds bridges between staff and clients and creates shared norms, (2) provides new functions and new roles, which enhance measures of self-worth, (3) reduces feelings of powerlessness and alienation, (4) leads to client change and/or develops staff capabilities.

Building Community

We "make war" on offenders. Police capture them and prisons lock them in. The conflict of interest is a real one; distrust and suspicion are well founded. The "war" holds for slum corners, where vigilance and aggressiveness insure survival. But conflict does not explain generalized contempt, stereotyping, panic, vindictiveness, exploitiveness, or cynicism. Staff do not require the working assumption that all clients (and prospective clients) are evil, threatening, or degenerate. Clients need not view all staff as malevolently arbitrary and tryannical. Inmates need not view fellow inmates as easy and inviting targets. But such notions derive from select skewed contacts. Police too often meet citizens only as adversaries; inmates too often meet guards only as confiners and punishers; they often see peers only as gang members or nonmembers. To balance such contacts we need other encounters that feature more reconcilable concerns and more collaborative links.

Converging interests are also real. Given expanding crime rates, agencies have no stake in promoting business; and, obviously, suspects and inmates have no stake in proliferated contact with criminal justice agencies. In theory, clients and staff have a shared concern with rehabilitation goals. The challenge is to create mechanisms that permit reciprocal interests to surface. Clients resist treatment that is imposed on them; treatment is withheld where it is resisted. But such cycles may be broken by "contractual" programs that permit clients to set their own treatment goals, allow them to engage in self help, and provide support that is invited by them [176]. Although staff-client mutuality can never be absolute (because staff are not seen as rehabilitation candidates) some teaming of staff and clients for rehabilitation is possible. It is also possible to use staff-inmate "linkers," such as rehabilitated clients, former clients, or indigenous paraprofessionals [175].

A possible convergence exists also in the area of humanitarian values. No one has a rational stake in aggravating the client suffering that is inevitably associated with arrest and imprisonment. No one profits where a suspect loses touch with his family or an inmate is terrorized. No one gains from brutal acts by clumsy staff. While protecting one's peers provides safety in the short run, it subverts morale and decreases efficiency in the long run. The consequences of violence document the need for generating new norms that recognize a shared interest in reducing exploitation and brutality. If necessary, peer and staff violence-reduction efforts can be separately initiated. And it might help if we make certain that punishment is not invoked where reform of violent men is possible.

Feedback and Self-esteem

Offenders and inmates are generally unloved. Less obviously, so are police and prison staff. Polls show respect for police, but officers see little evidence of it in their personal lives. Most contacts with citizens tend to be impersonal and brief. Off the job, police tend to socialize with each other and to conceal their identity from the general public.

Prison guards are less well regarded than police. Correctional budgets are low, and prisons are treated as necessary evils. Sympathetic portrayals of guards in the media are rare or nonexistent. TV shows have used patrolmen, detectives, and firemen as their heroes, but no prison guards.

There is no mystery about the conversion experiences of guard counsellors or guards-as-problem-solvers. A man who lives with public disdain and client contempt, and who discharges menial functions in a military chain, has a self-esteem vacuum. And guards—unlike police officers and inmate-bullies—cannot resort to "teaching respect" or to violence, to raise their status. The former is precluded by monitored rules, while the latter is rarely called for. Where violence exists, danger is real. Although guards may feel useful in riots, their dominant reaction is apt to be fear.

Where agencies experiment with service functions, they meet improved public acceptance. Even modest efforts provide citizen esteem. Police family crisis management teams may be called back by citizens for noncrisis advice. Inmate toy drives can bring warm correspondence between orphans and inmates.

Such positive reactions can reduce cynicism, and can raise self-esteem. The inmate Santa Claus and the officer who prevents an eviction are likely to generate more self-respect and less cynicism than either man seeing himself wending a self-contained way through hostile jungles. The need for positive feedback, hidden behind manly facades, explains the inmates's mysterious willingness to endure risk in pharmaceutical experiments, and the otherwise pragmatic officer's altruistic involvement in police athletic leagues.

Service activity, however, feeds more than egos. It gives men positive roles, which temper negative roles. The consumer-protecting officer and the inmate-counselor are likely to become more compassionate men. The stance that evolves can transfer to other functions. For police, it broadens the range for nonadversary interactions with citizens. For offenders, it is potentially resocializing. Pearl and Riessman [137] provide a fascinating example in a program that involved delinquent youths working as nursery aides. The role resocialized the youths by affording them unique opportunities to rehearse effective nontough, nonmacho conduct. The diluting of manly facades through helping roles can similarly reduce violence potential elsewhere.

To insure the transfer value of helping roles, they must be systemically integrated. The inmate-tutor or inmate-toy maker may boost his ego with extracurricular rape threats if his tutoring or toy making smacks among his peers of "finking" or of "sissy" conduct. Compartmentalized involvements may be coopted by macho values (as in inmate government efforts) or may produce organizational ghettoes (as in police community relations units). If caring and helping are to become stable instruments of self-esteem, they must be major organizational themes. This point has been made for police by the ABA recommendations for a positive service reward system, and is shown in prisons by positive peer cultures and other treatment milieus [185].

Reducing Alienation

Suspects tell us they are "harassed" by police; police charge they are "disrespected" or "handcuffed"; inmates claim that guards brutalize them; guards see themselves "treated worse than inmates." As descriptions of the system, such statements distort. As views of self, they are painfully valid.

The problem is the familiar one of alienation. Men feel that others do them wrong, with support from the world at large. Offenders "know" that the decks are stacked against them, and so do police; inmates feel powerless, but so do guards. The shared image is one of an overwhelming all-pervasive "System" that stifles creative expression, thought, and action. This dehumanizing "It" is a well-worn myth; it greets us among bored teenagers, disaffected assembly workers, and protest voters. It is the summary of a person's sense of frustration.

It is not surprising that our inmates and suspects—men who are deprived of freedom—should assign to our staff malevolently emasculating roles; nor is it surprising that police, who face hostility in citizens, should view citizens as ill-disposed. It is not even surprising—when we think about it—that conspiratorial nuances should sharpen such perspectives. What is really remarkable is that the perspectives of opposing groups are reciprocally linked. The inmate who defines himself "harassed" and is listened to, reinforces the custodial view that the "system" favors inmate interests. By the same token, custody's fear brings opposition to inmate "free speech," which undergirds inmate perspectives of systemic "oppression." "Never talk to a screw (or con)" reinforces stereotypes that feature strong, hostile organized groups.

Such cycles can be broken by actions such as "service" moves, which can disconfirm the alienated premises of opposing camps. A custodial union that includes good inmate food in contract demands creates doubts about its anti-inmate stance. A guard union that becomes concerned about guard brutality guarantees (after some puzzlement) a reduction in inmate alienation. The difficulty is only that such a move requires that one fearful and defensive faction first abandon its strongly motivated alienated stance.

But this difficulty is surmountable. Joint "service" efforts of any kind can provide a start. Guards and inmates who work together on building Christmas toys, or on improving the prison library, or in arranging a "fathers' day picnic" for children, can begin to sense their shared humanity. This can attenuate defensive solidarity norms that ultimately give violent guards and inmates their immunity and cover.

Building New Roles

Men who rely on extrinsic rewards are tied to pressures. Even where job discretion is wide, the press to "play it safe" is enormous. In human services work, this translates into formalism for staff and conformity for clients. It brings—at best— short-term or surface compliance.

Passive roles insure that ego needs are discharged extraorganizationally, that men seek self-esteem outside the organization or through extracurricular efforts within the organization. The alienated officer is thus more apt to feed his ego by "teaching respect" or by gathering "real life" material for war stories. And we must expect inmate predation in self-esteem vacuums, where young prisoners, like their peers on the street, have no sources of self-esteem, and no ways of gaining a sense of competence [33].

To revitalize an organization means to stimulate participation.[a] This need not be done to promote democracy, but to create commitment to organizational goals, because we know that those who are involved at the inception of a program gain meaning from its closure and implementation. Men work where they have a stake in succeeding. They achieve because they see a reason to, not because someone else does [17].

We have reviewed several instances in which the impact of participation on criminal justice reform has been dramatic. We have seen police critique the work of fellow police, and inmates voluntarily "handcuffed" to apprehensive fellow inmates. Such results are not achieved by decree. They occur where police officers *originate* peer panels and inmates *design* restraint measures. They occur where rank and file face a problem, work out a solution to it, and implement the solution.

Prison guards usually are traditionalists because their job is thus most tangibly defined [35]. But no meaningful prison reform is possible without rank-and-file involvement, and no guard involvement is likely where we assume, at the outset, that guards are dinosaurs. Men treated as impediments to change are apt to act the part.

Possibly only one out of ten guards might spontaneously welcome a new role as helper, or resocializer, of inmates. An additional eight guards might have an open mind on the subject, but there is no avenue to determine this fact. Until

---

[a]For prisons, this point has been made by the Corrections Task Force of the 1973 President's Commission, as Standard 14.7, "Participatory Management" [95, pp. 485–86].

new opportunities for change are created, the mental health oriented guard must discretely do what he can. And eight (or 800) potentially humane guards must follow custodial routine as the only option that is available to them.

The same point holds for inmates. We *assume* that inmates insist on doing "their own time." We arrange the situation for them to do time. Occasionally, a man proves the exception to our rules—he listens to a fellow inmate with concern, or he approaches a potential aggressor to dissuade him. In ambiguous special statuses (such as that of inmate nurse) some inmates may play unscheduled helpful roles. Other inmates must do their own time. Although the potential for community may be just as strong in San Quentin or at Walpole as it was in Makarenko's Gorky Colony, no evidence of the potential can become available if we do not defy self-fulfilling assumptions by setting up appropriate change vehicles.

Our conception of the world is limited by "What Is. We "know" police are not social workers, and we are absolutely right. A poll could confirm that self-respecting patrolmen would resign in a body ift they were rechristened "social workers." But these same officers can generate family crisis units, conflict management units, landlord tenant units, and consumer protection programs. Having generated such programs, they can cheerfully implement them, run them, and man them [179]. Individually, officers act superbly in "social work" encounters. They prevent suicides, reduce fear, settle disputes, make referrals; they comfort the sick or dying; they humor alcoholics, children, psychotics. They do what they do unselfconsciously, waiting for "real police work" to come along. And there is no reward for their work. It draws no headlines, medals, locker room acclaim. Catching burglars does.

Yet too few burglars get caught for victims to feel safe and for burglars to feel deterred. Too few burglars get caught for police to obtain a sense of pride. What police do obtain is a "cops and robbers" view of policing. Such a view highlights police functions that are static, and that cannot increase job satisfaction, public acceptance, and officer competence.

The situation is different where police departments highlight service functions. While burglars are elusive, community needs are not. Needs are, moreover, most acute where police stock is most depreciated, and the most likely consumers of positive police service are those who now see the police in "stop and frisk" terms.

The skill development potential of human service activity is great. To be effective, the peace keeper must develop, test, and improve interpersonal approaches, strategies, and ways of relating to diverse publics. While the enforcer's acumen in deploying stakeouts or judo holds has limited transfer value, interpersonal skills apply to traditional enforcement and custody work, and increase its effectiveness.

We may recall that Bard's FCI Unit members—beyond improving their conflict-reducing and arbitration skills—expanded their behavioral repertoire. It stands to reason that California's inmate grievance managers and Maxwell Jones' patients learned (as they were supposed to) constructive approaches to interpersonal dealings. This consideration is uniquely relevant to the resocialization of violence, because the nonviolent behavioral options of violent men are frequently primitive and few [178].

Beyond improved skill is improved self-esteem. Men with more options feel more secure. They are less apt to be trapped into responding to challenges, taunts, baiting, and "tests" of "manhood." They are less likely than some of our staff and our clients to play unseemly games with unworthy opponents at everyone else's expense.

References

1. American Bar Association, Project of Standards for Criminal Justice, *The Urban Police Function*. New York: Institute of Judicial Administration, 1973.

2. American Correctional Association, *Causes, Preventive Measures and Methods of Controlling Riots and Disturbances in Correctional Institutions*. Washington: October 1970.

3. ——, *Correction Officers Training Guide*, College Park, Md.: 1959, pp. 16–18.

4. American Psychiatric Association, *Task Force on Clinical Aspects of the Violent Individual* (Report No. 8).

5. Ball-Rokeach, Sandra J., "The Legitimization of Violence," in Short, J.F., and Wolfgang, M.E., eds., *Collective Violence.* Chicago: Aldine, 1972, pp. 100–111.

6. Bandura, A., *Principles of Behavior Modification,* New York: Holt, Rinehart & Winston, 1969.

7. Bard, M., *Training Police as Specialists in Family Crisis Intervention,* Final Report to OLEA. New York: CUNY, 1970a.

8. ——, *Police Management of Conflicts Among People,* Final Report to NILECJ. New York: Psychological Center, CUNY, 1970b.

9. Barker E.T., Billings, R., and McLaughlin, A.J., "The Total Encounter Capsule," National Scientific Planning Council of the Canadian Mental Health Association, Twenty-first Annual Meeting, Toronto, March 14, 1969.

10. Barker, E.T., and Mason, M.H., "Buber Behind Bars," *Canadian Psychiatric Association Journal,* 1969, *13,* 61–71.

11. Barker, E.T., Mason, M.H., and Walls, J., *Protective Pairings in Treatment Milieux: Handcuffs for Mental Patients.* Ontario Hospital, Penetanguishene, undated.

12. Bayh, Senator B., *Our Nation's Schools–a Report Card: "A" in School Violence and Vandalism,* Preliminary Report of the Subcommittee to Investigate Juvenile Delinquency, to the Committee on the Judiciary, U.S. Senate, April 1975. Washington: U.S. Government Printing Office, 1975.

13. Bittner, E., "Police Discretion in Emergency Apprehension of Mentally Ill Persons," *Social Problems,* 1967(a), *14,* 278–292.

14. ——, "The Police in Skid-Row: A Study in Peace-Keeping," *American Sociological Review,* 1967(b), *32,* 699–715.

15. Bloch, P., and Anderson, Deborah, *Policewomen on Patrol: Final Report.* Washington: Police Foundation, 1974.

16. Bloch, P., Anderson, Deborah, and Gervais, Pamela, *Policewomen on Patrol.* Washington: Police Foundation, 1973.

17. Blumberg, P., *Industrial Democracy: The Sociology of Participation.* New York: Schocken Books, 1973.

18. Boslow, H. et al., "Methods and Experiences in Group Treatment of Defective Delinquents in Maryland," *The Journal of Social Therapy,* 1969, *7* (Patuxent reprint), 11 pp.

19. Boslow, H.M., and Kandel, A., "Administrative Structure and Therapeutic Climate," *The Prison Journal,* 1966, *46,* 23-31.

20. Boslow, H.M., and Kohlmeyer, W.A., "The Maryland Defective Delinquency Law: An Eight Year Follow-up," *American Journal of Psychiatry,* 1963, *120,* 118-124.

21. Boslow, H., and Manne, S.H., "Mental Health in Action, Treating Adult Offenders at Patuxent Institution," *Crime and Delinquency,* 1966, 22-28.

22. Boslow, H., Rosenthal, D. and Gliedman, L.H., "The Maryland Defective Delinquency Law, Psychiatric Implications for the Treatment of Antisocial Disorders under the Law." Jessup, Maryland: Patuxent Institution, Reprint January 1972, 5-13.

23. Briggs, D.L., and Dowling, J.M., "The Correctional Officer as a Consultant: An Emerging Role in Penology," *American Journal of Correction,* May–June 1964, 28-31.

24. Brown, W., *Police and Crime Prevention,* MPA Thesis, New York University, 1948.

25. Buffum, P.C., *Homosexuality in Prisons,* NILECJ Monograph, Washington: U.S. Government Printing Office, February 1972.

26. Calhoun, F. (Associate Director, Superintendent, Patuxent), Personal Communication, 1975.

27. California Department of Corrections, *CDC Stabbing Incident Comparisons* (Memoranda to Director of Corrections). Sacramento: April 8, 1974, July 10, 1974; (mimeo).

28. California Department of Corrections, Research Division, *A Study of Trends Among Newly Admitted Inmates, 1960, 1965, 1970, 1973.* Sacramento: 1974, mimeo.

29. ——, *Brief Analysis of Characteristics of Male Felon Inmates Designated as Aggressors in Stabbing Incidents.* Sacramento: May 1974 (mimeo).

30. Cheatwood, A.D., *Restrictive Labels in a Juvenile Correctional Setting.* Columbus: Program for the Study of Crime and Delinquency, Ohio State University, 1972.

31. Chevigny, P., *Police Power: Police Abuses in New York City,* New York: Pantheon, 1969.

32. Citizens Commission to Investigate Corporal Punishment in Junior High School 22, *Corporal Punishment and School Suspensions: A Case Study.* New York: Metropolitan Applied Research Center, 1974.

33. Cohen, A.K., *Delinquent Boys: The Culture of the Gang.* Glencoe: Free Press, 1955.

34. Committee on the Judiciary, House of Representatives, Subcommittee No. 3, Hearings: *Prisoner's Representation,* November 10, 11–December 2, 1971. Washington: U.S. Government Printing Office, 1972.

35. Cressey, D., "Prison Organizations," Chapter 24 in March, J.G., ed., *Handbook of Organizations,* pp. 1023–1070. New York: Rand McNally, 1965.

36. Cumming, Elaine, Cumming, I. and Edell, Laura, "Policeman as Philosopher, Guide and Friend," *Social Problems,* 1965, *12,* 276–286.

37. Daley R., "The Myth of the Killer Cop," *New York,* August 13, 1973, 25–33.

38. Daniels, Sammy (Petitioner) vs. Boslow, Harold M. (Director of Patuxent Institution-Respondent), Trial Court Opinion, The Constitutional Application of The Maryland Defective Delinquent Law. In the Circuit Court for Prince George's County, Maryland, December 15, 1965.

39. Davis. A.J., "Sexual Assaults in the Philadelphia Prison System and Sheriff's Vans," *Trans-Action,* 1968, *6,* 8–16.

40. *Defective Delinquency Statute,* Article 31B, Annotated Code of the Public General Laws of Maryland, 1972 Cumulative Supplement, (Jessup, Maryland: Patuxent Institution, Reprint, October 1973, 18 pp.).

41. Denenberg, R.V., and Denenberg, Tia, "Prison Grievance Procedures," *Corrections Magazine,* 1975, *1,* 29 ff.

42. Deutsch, M., *The Resolution of Conflict: Constructive and Destructive Processes.* New Haven: Yale University Press, 1973.

43. Doering, C.R., ed., *A Report on the Development of Penological Treatment at Norfolk Prison Colony in Massachusetts* (with contributions by W.H. Commons, T. Yahkub, and E. Powers). New York: Bureau of Social Hygiene, 1940.

44. Ellis, D., *Violence in Prisons,* Lexington, Mass.: Lexington Books, D.C. Heath and Co., in press.

45. Ellis, D.H., Grasmick, G., and Gilman, B., "Violence in Prisons: A Sociological Analysis," *American Journal of Sociology,* 1974, *80,* 16–43.

46. Fairweather, G.W. et al., *Community Life for the Mentally Ill: An Alternative to Institutional Care.* Chicago: Aldine, 1969.

47. Freud, S., *A General Introduction to Psychoanalysis,* New York: Permabooks, 1953, Twenty-Seventh Lecture: "Transference," pp. 438–455.

48. ——, "Analysis, Terminable and Interminable," in *Therapy and Technique.* New York: Collier Books, 1963a, pp. 233–272.

49. ——, "Further Recommendations in the Technique of Psychoanaly-

sis: On Beginning the Treatment. The Operation of the First Communications. The Dynamics of the Cure," in *Therapy and Technique*. New York: Collier Books, 1963b.

50. Fromm-Reichmann, Frieda, *Principles of Intensive Psychotherapy*. Chicago: University of Chicago Press, 1950.

51. Gagon, J.H., "The Social Meaning of Prison Homosexuality," *Federal Probation*, 1968, *32*, 1ff.

52. Glaser, D., *The Effectiveness of a Prison and Parole System*. Indianapolis: Bobbs-Merril, 1964.

53. Grant, J.D., "Management of Conflict in Correctional Institutions," *"Medical Care of Prisoners and Detainees."* Amsterdam: Ciba Foundation, 1973 Symposium #16 (new series), pp. 183-192.

54. Grosz, H.J., Stern, H., and Feldman, E., "A Study of Delinquent Girls who Participated in and Who Abstained from Participating in a Riot," *American Journal of Psychiatry*, 1969, *125*, 1370-1380.

55. Guenther, A.J., *Violence in Correctional Institutions: A Study of Assaults*, American Correctional Association, Annual Meetings, 1974.

56. Halfon, A., and Steadman, H., "The Baxtrom Women: A Four-year Follow-up of Behavior Patterns, *"Psychiatric Quarterly*, 1972, *45*, 1-10.

57. Harding, R.W., and Fahey, R., "Killings by Chicago Police, 1969-1970: An Empirical Study," *South California Law Review*, 1973, *46*, 284-315.

58. Heise, W.F., *The California Medical Facility Stress Assessment Unit*, Memorandum, April 19, 1965.

59. Hoobler, R.L., and McQueeney, J.A., *A Question of Height*, Mimeograph Report, San Diego Police Department, San Diego, California, undated.

60. Huffman, A.V., "Problems Precipitated by Sexual Approaches on Youthful First Offenders," *Journal of Social Therapy*, 1961, *7*, 216-222.

61. Ingraham, B.L., "Will Legal Relief for Inmates Prevent Violence in Correctional Institutions?" in *Prevention of Violence in Correctional Institutions*, Criminal Justice Monograph, U.S. Department of Justice, NILCJ, LEAA. Washington: U.S. Government Printing Office, 1973.

62. Irwin, J., *The Felon*, Englewood Cliffs, N.J.: Prentice Hall, 1970.

63. Jacobs, J.B., and Retsky, H.G. "Prison Guard," *Urban Life*, 1975, *4*, 5-29.

64. Jaman, Dorothy M., *Characteristics of Violent Prisoners (San Quentin, 1960)*. Sacramento: California Department of Corrections, Research Report No. 22, June 1966.

65. Johnson, E., "Sociology of Confinement: Assimilation and the Prison Rat," *Journal of Criminal Law, Criminology and Police Science*, 1961, *51*, 228-233.

66. Jones, M., *The Therapeutic Community*. New York: Basic Books, 1953.

67. Kalogerakis, M.G., "The Assaultive Psychiatric Patient," *Psychiatric Quarterly*, 1971, *45*, 372-381.

68. Katsampes, P., *Changing Correction Officers through Decision Making Training Sessions*. Albany: School of Criminal Justice, 1972.

69. Kirkham, G.L., *The Limits of Police Discretion in Lower Class versus Middle Class Environments*, Annual Meetings, American Society of Criminology, 1974.

70. Kobler, A.L., "Police Homicide in a Democracy," *Journal of Social Issues*, 1975, *31*, 163-184.

71. Kozol, H.L., Boucher, R.J., and Garofalo, R.F., "The Diagnosis and Treatment of Dangerousness," *Crime and Delinquency*, 1972, *18*, 371-392.

72. Krech, D., and Crutchfield, R.S., *Theory and Problems in Social Psychology*. New York: McGraw-Hill, 1948.

73. Lewin, K., "Field Theory and Experiment in Social Psychology: Concepts and Methods," *American Journal of Sociology*, 1939, *44*, 868-896.

74. ———, "Frontiers in Group Dynamics," in *Field Theory in Social Science*. New York: Harper, 1951, pp. 188-238.

75. ———, *Resolving Social Conflicts*. New York: Harper, 1948.

76. Lindner, R.M., "Sexual Behavior in Penal Institutions," in Deutsch, A., ed., *Sex Habits of American Men*. New York: Prentice-Hall, 1948.

77. Lohman, J.D., *The Police and Minority Groups*. Chicago: The Chicago Park District, 1947.

78. Makarenko, A.S., *The Road to Life: The Epic of Education*, 3 vols. Moscow: Foreign Language Publishing House, 1955.

79. Manne, S., "The Relationship Between Institutional Treatment and Parole," *Official Newsletter and Journal of the American Association of Correctional Psychologists, Affiliate of the American Correctional Association*, 1969, *3* (Patuxent reprint), 5 pp.

80. Manne, S., Kandel, A., and Rosenthal, D., "Differences Between Performance IQ and Verbal IQ in a Severely Sociopathic Population," *Journal of Clinical Psychology*, 1962, *XVIII*, 96-97.

81. ———, "The Relationship between Performance Minus Verbal Scores and Extraversion in a Severely Sociopathic Population," *Clinical Psychology*, 1963, *XIX* (1), 73-77.

82. Mathiesen, T., *The Defences of the Weak: A Sociological Study of a Norwegian Correctional Institution*. London: Tavistock, 1965.

83. May, E., "Prison Ombudsmen in America," *Corrections Magazine*, 1975, *1*, 45 ff.

84. McCleery, R.H., "The Government Process and Informal Social Control," in Cressey, D.R., *The Prison: Studies in Institutional Organization and Change*. New York: Holt, Rinehart and Winston, 1961, pp. 149-188.

85. McNamara, J.H., "Uncertainties of Police Work: The Relevance of

Police Recruits' Background and Training," in Bordua, D.J., ed., *The Police: Six Sociological Essays*. New York: Wiley, 1967.

86. Megargee, E.I., "Undercontrolled and Overcontrolled Personality Types in Extreme Antisocial Aggression," *Psychological Monographs*, 1966, *80* (3, Whole No. 611).

87. Meister, J.S., "A Visit to Patuxent: 'Participation is Voluntary . . .'" *Hastings Center Report 5*, February 1975, 37–38.

88. Metropolitan Applied Research Center, *Corporal Punishment and School Suspensions: A Case Study*, MARC Monograph #2, October 1974.

89. Milgram, S., *Obedience to Authority: An Experimental View*. New York: Harper and Row, 1974.

90. Milton, Catherine H., *Women in Policing*. Washington: The Police Foundation, March 1972.

91. Mintz, Ellen, Sandler, Georgette B., and Prager, J., *From Police Force to Police Service: The Response to Violence*, Paper presented at Annual Meetings of the American Society of Criminology, Chicago, 1974.

92. Mitford, J., *Kind and Usual Punishment: The Prison Business*. New York: Knopf, 1973.

93. Morris, Norval, *The Future of Imprisonment*. Chicago: The University of Chicago Press, 1974.

94. Mueller, P.F.C., Toch, H., and Molof, M.F., *Report to the Task Force to Study Violence in Prisons*, August 1965. Sacramento: California Department Corrections, 1965.

95. National Advisory Commission on Criminal Justice Standards and Goals, Task Force on Corrections, *Corrections*. Washington: U.S. Government Printing Office, 1973.

96. ——, Task Force Report,.*Police*, Washington, D.C., U.S. Government Printing Office, 1973.

97. New York Department of Corrections, *Record of Use of Physical Force: Annual Report*, for 1973 (Tables).

98. New York Department of Corrections, *N.Y. State Department of Correctional Services Employee Handbook*.

99. New York State Special Commission on Attica, *Attica*. New York: Bantam Books, 1972.

100. *New York Times*, February 2, 1971.

101. ——, February 7, 1971.

102. ——, November 28, 1971.

103. ——, November 9, 1972.

104. ——, January 31, 1973.

105. ——, February 7, 1973.

106. ——, February 11, 1973.

107. ——, June 4, 1973.

108. ——, June 11, 1973.

129

109. ——, June 14, 1973.
110. ——, June 17, 1973.
111. ——, July 25, 1973.
112. ——, August 26, 1973.
113. ——, September 5, 1973.
114. ——, October 1, 1973.
115. ——, November 23, 1973.
116. ——, December 5, 1973.
117. ——, January 17, 1974.
118. ——, February 8, 1974.
119. ——, May 13, 1974.
120. ——, June 13, 1974.
121. ——, June 24, 1974.
122. ——, July 15, 1974.
123. ——, August 13, 1974.
124. ——, August 27, 1974.
125. ——, September 2, 1974.
126. ——, September 3, 1974.
127. ——, September 12, 1974.
128. ——, September 17, 1974.
129. ——, September 21, 1974.
130. ——, September 23, 1974.
131. ——, December 12, 1974.
132. ——, January 1, 1975.
133. Niederhoffer, A., *Behind the Shield: The Police in Urban Society.* New York: Doubleday, Anchor, 1969.
134. O'Leary, V., *Symposium on Conflict Resolution and Negotiation in Prisons.* Hackensack: National Council on Crime and Delinquency, 1973.
135. OSS Assessment Staff, *The Assessment of Men.* New York: Rinehart, 1948.
136. Pasternack, S.A., ed., *Violence and Victims.* New York: Spectrum Books, 1975.
137. Pearl, A., and Riessman, F., *New Careers for the Poor: The Nonprofessional in Human Service.* New York: The Free Press, 1965.
138. President's Commission on Law Enforcement and Administration of Justice, Task Force Report, *Corrections.* Washington: U.S. Government Printing Office, 1967.
139. ——, *The Police.* Washington: U.S. Government Printing Office, 1967.
140. Radelet, L.A., *The Police and The Community.* Beverly Hills: Glencoe Press, 1973.
141. Raphael, A., "Ombudsmen and Prisons: The European Experience," *Correction Magazine,* 1975, *1*, 56-57.
142. Redl, F., "Improvement Panic and Improvement Shock," in *When We*

Deal with Children. New York: The Free Press, 1966, pp. 95-124.

143. Redl, F., and Wineman, D., *Children Who Hate: The Disorganization and Breakdown of Behavior Controls.* New York: Collier Books, 1962.

144. Reiss, A.J., "Police Brutality: Answers to Key Questions," in Lipsky, M., ed., *Law and Order: Police Encounters.* Chicago: Aldine, 1970.

145. ——, *The Police and the Public.* New Haven: Yale, 1971.

146. Reiwald, P., *Society and its Criminals.* New York: International University Press, 1950.

147. Robin, G.D., "Justifiable Homicide by Police Officers," *Journal of Criminal Law, Criminology and Police Science,* 1963, *54,* 225-231.

148. Robinson, J., Address on "Defective Delinquency," General Assembly of the States Governments, December 5, 1958.

149. Rubin, B., "Prediction of Dangerousness in Mental Ill Criminals," *Archives of General Psychiatry,* 1972, *27,* 397-402.

150. Rummel, B., "The Right of Law Enforcement Officers to Use Deadly Force to Effect and Arrest," *New York Law Forum,* 1968, *14,* 749-762.

151. Safer, J.G., "Deadly Weapons in the Hands of Police Officers, On Duty and Off Duty," *Journal of Urban Law,* 1971, *49,* pp. 565-579.

152. San Francisco Police Department. Internal Memorandum, 1959-1963, dated 10-12-64, mimeo.

153. *San Quentin News,* June 13, 1975.

154. Scharf, P., and Kohlberg, L., "Inmate Perceptions of Institutional and Legal Norms: A Cognitive-Developmental Perspective," Paper presented at American Psychological Association, September 1974.

155. Sellin, T., "Prison Homicides," in Sellin, T., ed., *Capital Punishment.* New York: Harper and Row, 1967, pp. 154-160.

156. Shah, S.A., "Some Interactions of Law and Mental Health in the Handling of Social Deviance," *Catholic University Law Review,* 1974, *4,* 674-719.

157. Sherman, L.W., Milton, C.H., and Kelley, T.V., *Team Policing: Seven Case Studies.* Washington: Police Foundation, 1973.

158. Shrom, S., "Authority: One Aspect of the Correctional Worker-Client Relationship," *Canadian Journal of Criminology,* 1972, *14,* 182 ff.

159. Skelton, W.D., "Prison Riot Assaulters vs. Defenders," *Archives of General Psychiatry,* 1969, *21,* 359-362.

160. Skolnick, J.H., *Justice Without Trial: Law Enforcement in a Democratic Society.* Boston: Little, Brown, 1970.

161. Smith, R.J., "The Use of Deadly Force by a Peace Officer in the Apprehension of a Person in Flight," *University of Pittsburgh Law Review,* 1959, *21,* 132-141.

162. South Carolina Department of Corrections, Collective Violence Research Project, *Collective Violence in Correctional Institutions: A Search for Causes.* Columbia, S.C.: 1973a.

163. South Carolina Department of Corrections, *Inmate Grievance Procedures,* Columbia, S.C.: 1973b.

164. Steadman, H.J., "The Determination of Dangerousness in New York," Paper presented at 1974 Annual Meetings of American Psychiatric Association, Detroit, Michigan.

165. ——, "The Psychiatrist as a Conservative Agent of Social Control," *Social Problems,* 1972, *20,* 263-271.

166. Steadman, H.J., and Halfon, A., "The Baxtrom Patients: Backgrounds and Outcomes," *Seminars in Psychiatry,* 1971, *3,* 376-386.

167. Steadman, H.J., and J.J. Cocozza, *Careers of the Criminally Insane.* Lexington, Mass: Lexington Books, D.C. Heath and Co., 1974.

168. Sturup, G.K., *Treating the Untreatable.* Baltimore: John Hopkins, 1968.

169. Stutsman, L.M. et al., The Task Force to Study Violence, *Report and Recommendations,* May 1974. Sacramento: Department of Corrections, 1974.

170. Sykes, G., *The Society of Captives.* New York: Atheneum, 1966.

171. Symonds, M., "The Emotional Hazards of Police Work," *Newsletter, Academy of Police Science,* May 1969, pp. 1-8.

172. Szasz, T.S., *The Myth of Mental Illness: Foundations of a Theory of Personal Conduct.* New York: Dell Publishing, 1961.

173. Thornberry, T.P., and Jacoby, J.E., "The Use of Discretion in a Maximum Security Hospital: The Dixon Case," Paper presented at 1974 Annual Meetings of the American Society of Criminology, Chicago, Illinois.

174. *Times Union* (Albany), December 4, 1973.

175. Toch, H., *Men in Crisis: Human Breakdowns in Prison.* Chicago: Aldine, 1975.

176. ——, "The Care and Feeding of Typologies and Labels," *Federal Probation,* 1970, *34,* 15-19.

177. ——, The Delinquent as a Poor Loser. *Seminars in Psychiatry,* 1971, *3,* 386-399.

178. ——, *Violent Men: An Inquiry into the Psychology of Violence.* Chicago: Aldine, 1969.

179. Toch, H., Grant, J.D., and Galvin, R., *Agents of Change: A Study in Police Reform.* Cambridge, Mass.: Schenkman, 1975.

180. Tong, J.E., and MacKay, G.W., "A Statistical Follow-up of Mental Defectives of Dangerous and Violent Propensities," *British Journal of Delinquency,* 1959, *9,* 276-284.

181. U.S. Department of HEW, National Center for Health Statistics, *Vital Statistics of the U.S., 1968,* Vol. 2, *Mortality,* Part A, 1972.

182. U.S. Department of Justice, Federal Bureau of Investigations, *Uniform Crime Reports,* 1971, August 1972.

183. U.S. Department of Justice LEAA, *Sourcebook of Criminal Justice Statistics,* 1973. Washington: U.S. Government Printing Office, 1973.

184. U.S. Riot Commission, *Report of the National Advisory Commission on Civil Disorders.* New York: Bantam Books, 1968.

185. Vorrath, H.H., and L.K. Brendthro, *Positive Peer Culture,* Chicago: Aldine, 1974.

186. Walker, D., ed., *Rights in Conflict: "The Chicago Police Riot,"* Official Report to the National Commission on the Causes and Prevention of Violence. New York: New American Library, 1968.

187. Walle, L., and Morris, P.L., "Speech and Hearing Research and Therapy with Sociopathic Criminals." American Speech and Hearing Association Convention, Speech and Language Disorders in Psychiatric Patients Section, November 22, 1966.

188. Ward, J.L., "Homosexual Behavior of the Institutionalized Delinquent," *Psychiatric Quarterly Supplement,* 1958, *32,* 301-314.

189. Wenk, E.A., Robinson, J.O., and Smith, G.W., "Can Violence be Predicted?" *Crime and Delinquency,* 1972, *18,* 393-402.

190. Wertham, C., and Piliavin, I., "Gang Members and the Police," in Bordua, D.J., ed., *The Police: Six Sociological Essays.* New York: Wiley, 1967.

191. Westley, W.A., *Violence and the Police: A Sociological Study of Law, Custom, and Morality.* Boston: The M.I.T. Press, 1970.

192. White, L., Krumholz, V.W., and Fink, L., "The Adjustment of Criminally Insane Persons to a Civil Mental Hospital," *Mental Hygiene,* 1969, *53,* 34-40.

193. Wilkins, L.T., "Current Aspects of Penology: Directions for Corrections," *Proceedings of the American Philosophical Society,* 1974, *118,* 235-245.

194. Wilson, J.Q., *Varieties of Police Behavior: The Management of Law and Order in Eight Communities.* Cambridge: Harvard University Press, 1968.

195. Wolfgang, M.E., "Corrections and the Violent Offender," *Annals, American Academy of Political and Social Science,* 1969, *381,* 119-124.

196. Wolfgang, M., and Ferracuti, F., *The Subculture of Violence: Towards an Integrated Theory of Criminology.* London: Tavistock, 1967.

197. Wolfson, W., Untitled paper about prison homicides, Presentation at Conference on Violence in Prisons, Durham, New Hampshire, May 31, 1975.

198. Yinger, M., "Contraculture and Subculture," *American Sociological Review,* 1960, *25,* 625-635.

199. Ziegler, H., "Prison: What's it all About?" *Society,* July-August 1974, 67-69.

Index

Academies, police, 21. *See also* Training
Adjudication, of defective delinquency, 97; grievance, 67
Administration, police, 33–36; prison, 65
Airports, security measures at, 12
Alcohol, 29; and violence, 83
Alienation, 109, 111; reduction of, 118–119
American Bar Association (ABA), Police Standards Manual of, 36
American Civil Liberties Union (ACLU), 21
American Correctional Association, standards of, 100
Amnesty, demands for, 66
Appeals, inmate, 71
Arbitration, of riots, 66; of special grievances, 71
Armament, police, 12
Arrests, 17, 27
Assaults, inmate, 48–58; on policemen, 16. *See also* Violence
Attitudes, toward doctors, 57; toward police, 17
Authority, perceived defiance of, 22–23; in prison, 66; resentment of, 88. *See also* Roles

Backlash, 41
Bard, Morton, 42
Barker, E.T., 104, 105
Borland, John, 46
Boslow, H., 95, 96, 98, 99
Bow and Arrow Squad, 32
Briggs, D.L., 75
Brutality, charges of, 16; police, 22. *See also* Violence
Buffum, P.C., 62

California, penology surveys in, 48; prisons of, 55
California Medical Facility, Stress Assessment Unit at, 93
California Youth Authority (CYA), 71–72
Cawley, Commissioner, 43
Cheatwood, Adrian, 89, 90
Chevigny, Paul, 21, 22
Civil Rights, 7
Class, authority and, 22
Classification, decisions for, 106

Community, building of, 116; police relations with, 37–38; prison, 77–79; therapeutic, 103–106
Community relations, 7; police (PCR), 37–38
Conflict, generation of, 6–7; group, 115; prison management of, 65–79
Confrontations, police–citizen, 28. *See also* Relationships
Connecticut, ombudsman's role in, 70
Connecticut State Farm for Women, 78
Control, 34
Corporal punishment, in schools, 4
Corrections Officers Training Guide, 59
Councils, inmate, 76
Counseling, by prison officers, 75
Courts, and inmate grievances, 71
Cover-up, by inmates, 78; by prison guards, 74
Crises, of inmate populations, 61
Crisis intervention units, 41. *See also* Family Crisis Intervention
Custody, 113; v. therapy, 106
Cynicism, 110; of gang members, 23; police, 19, 21, 28, 29; reduction of, 117

Daley, R., 32, 34
Dangerousness, of inmates, 85; transactional nature of, 87–90
Davis, A.J., 62
Death penalty, in Pennsylvania, 58
Decarceration, 49, 50, 55, 115
Defensiveness, 108
Dehumanization, 64
Denenberg. R.V., 71, 72
Denenberg, Tia, 71, 72
Deterrence, in prison, 66
Detroit House of Corrections, 76
Discipline, and peer review panels, 39
Discrimination, 14
Disruption, 3
Doctors, attitudes toward, 57
Dowling, J.M., 75
Drunkenness, and violence, 83

Ego, male, 7. *See also* Manliness
Escalation, 57, 109

133

About the Author

Hans Toch is Professor of Psychology at the School of Criminal Justice, State University of New York at Albany. He received the Ph.D. (1955) from Princeton University. His published works include the following books: *Legal and Criminal Psychology, The Social Psychology of Social Movements, Social Perception: The Development of Inter-Personal Impressions, Violent Men: An Inquiry into the Psychology of Violence, Agents of Change: A Study in Police Reform,* and *Men in Crisis: Human Breakdowns in Prison.* Other publications include some 50 journal articles and 8 chapters in books. Professor Toch taught at Michigan State University from 1957 through 1968, was a visiting lecturer at Harvard University and a Fulbright Fellow in Norway. He is a fellow of the American Psychological Association.